CW00515228

THE LANGUAGE OF

This book explains baffling professional jargon in clear non-technical language and provides an easy-to-use A–Z index of specialised terminology.

Also in this series

THE LANGUAGE OF PHOTOGRAPHY

Mary Harwood

A STAR BOOK
published by
the Paperback Division of
W. H. ALLEN & Co. Ltd

A Star Book
Published in 1981
by the Paperback Division of
W. H. Allen & Co. Ltd
A Howard and Wyndham Company
44 Hill Street, London W1X 8LB

First published in the United States by
Running Press 1978 as the Running Press Glossary of
Photography Language

Copyright © 1978 Running Press

Printed in Great Britain by
The Anchor Press Ltd, Tiptree, Essex

ISBN 0 352 30897 4

This book is sold subject to the condition that it shall
not, by way of trade or otherwise, be lent,
re-sold, hired out or otherwise circulated without the
publisher's prior consent in any form of binding
or cover other than that in which it is published
and without a similar condition including this
condition being imposed on the subsequent purchaser.

Preface

Ever been stumped by a term in a photo magazine? Ever been confused by a camera salesman who is extolling the virtues of diodes? Would you like to know about how your camera works without getting a Ph.D. in physics? You're not alone.

In recent years there has been a tremendous increase in amateur and semi-amateur interest in the more complicated forms of photography. This, coupled with a mind-boggling increase in the technology of both picture-taking and picture-making, has created a serious language gap. For those of us who are not chemists or physicists, this glossary has been designed to help bridge that gap and fill a few of the chinks left by regular professional jargon.

I have tried to include as many versions of a term as are practical in those instances where there is more than one name for an item. Many photographic terms are popularly known by their trademark; in these instances, I have used both the trademark and the generic name for the object or process. Individual brand names of films and cameras have been excluded for the obvious reason that there is no end to them.

This glossary is not meant to make you a photographer—only your own work can do that. It could, however, put you on the right track and may even introduce you to new processes and items you never understood before.

The only other thing I have to say is, keep the bugs out of your darkroom and watch out for *Shirley*.

—*Mary Harwood*

NOTE: *Italics* are used to indicate that a term in a definition is defined elsewhere in the glossary.

AA cells. Small, thin batteries used to power an electronic flash gun. Often referred to as penlights.

Abbe number. Used to express the dispersive power of a lens, this number represents the relation of the angles of deviation and refraction of a lens and measures the difference in refraction of light of different colors.

Aberration. Blurrings or distortions of an image as a result of light rays imperfectly focused through a lens. These imperfections are almost always present in a lens to some degree and are categorized as spherical, aberration, coma, astigmatism and field curvature, distortion, and chromatic aberratiion.

AC unit. An electronic flash that operates on regular household current.

Accelerator. A chemical added to developer to speed up the initial slow reaction on the film emulsion. Accelerator works so well, though, that an additional chemical restrainer must be added to prevent overdevelopment.

Acetate filter. Used in enlargers between the condenser and negative to affect the contrast on variable contrast paper and to balance the enlarger light in color printing.

Achromat. A lens which has been corrected so that two different colors of light may be brought to the same focus. The other colors of light not brought to a focus in an achromat lens form the secondary spectrum for that lens. The colors usually dealt with in an anchromat lens are blue and green.

Acutance. The edge sharpness of a particle of the film emulsion. Acutance is used as a measure of the overall sharpness of a film. For instance, if a film has fine grain but low acutance, it will not produce a very clear image. Also called contour sharpness.

Adapter ring. A marvelous little device that lets you borrow lenses from your friends. Since each manufacturer designs his lenses for his camera body, mounts can differ drastically. An adapter ring allows a bayonet-mount lens to be used on a screw-mount camera body. One word of caution—when using an adapter ring, you usually lose your automatic meter coupling.

Additive process. A method used to mix colors of light. In this process, the primary colors are red, green, and blue light, which when mixed equally, appear as white light to the human eye. Other combinations of these primaries will produce almost all colors. The additive process formed the basis for early color photography and is the principle employed in color television. Modern photography uses the subtractive process—a method in which colors are taken away from white light to obtain mixes—as the basis for all color films.

Adjacency effect. Density variation at the edge of areas of different densities in a negative. When there is an increase in density at the edge, it is called border effect. A lessening of density is referred to as fringe effect.

Aerial perspective. The impression of distance perceived in outdoors photography. Distant objects, such as mountain ridges, appear lighter in color and gradually melt away in a blue haze. When this distortion is corrected by using haze filters, the clearer background seems much closer than it actually is because of a new distortion in aerial perspective caused by the filters.

Afocal adapter. Coupling ring used to mount a camera to the eyepiece of a telescope.

Afocal method. A procedure used to take pictures with a regular camera through a telescope. In the afocal method, the camera (with the lens focused to infinity) is attached directly to the eyepiece of the telescope, usually with an afocal adapter. The picture may then be shot directly through both the camera lens and the telescope.

Agitation. Moderate shaking, or agitation, during development of film or paper brings fresh developer in contact with the exposed surface. This ensures complete and even development of the light-sensitive particles.

Aim point. The point at which a color film is considered to have its optimum color balance. Most films are sold "green," that is, before they reach the aim point. This is done to prevent disappointing color rendition that can result if the film is stored at a shop or in a camera too long before processing.

Air brush. (1) A device used to spray paint on a photograph to alter the image. An air brush can be used to retouch details lost in development as well as to remove whole portions of a photograph. (2) To use an air brush.

Albada finder. A type of view finder that has the actual image size marked off with a white frame on a larger field.

Amber safelight. A dark yellow light used in darkrooms because it does not affect most printing paper.

Amberlith. Trademark for a yellow masking film manufactured by the Ulano Company for screening out parts of an image when using materials not sensitive to yellow light.

Ambient light. Light reflected on a subject from several directions or to the sides.

American Standards Association. See *ASA.*

Angle of deviation. The difference in the angle of a light ray after it has been refracted.

Angle of incidence. The angle of a light ray as it enters a lens. The angle of incidence determines the angle of refraction. If there is no angle of incidence—that is, if the light strikes the lens head-on—there is no refraction.

Angle of refraction. The amount that light bends as it passes through a medium of a specific density.

Anti-fog solution. Chemical used to remove fog from paper that has been struck by light.

Antihalation backing. A special light-absorbing coating or layer on film that reduces internal reflections. See under *Halation.*

Aperture. The hole formed by the diaphragm which regulates the amount of light passing through the lens.

Aperture setting. By varying the size of the opening of the diaphragm, the aperture setting can control the rate at which light enters the camera. Aperture settings are called f/stops or f/numbers.

Aplanat lens. A double lens that has been corrected for both coma and spherical aberrations. Developed independently in 1866 in Germany and England, this lens was widely used on cameras well into the 1900s. Dubbed aplanat by the German inventor, this lens was also called the Rapid Rectilinear in English-speaking countries.

Apochromat. See under *Secondary spectrum.*

ASA. American Standards Association. This is a numerical rating that denotes a film's sensitivity to light, or its "speed." As the number rises, the amount of light needed to produce a normal image decreases. Speeds ranging from ASA 20 to 50, such as in most color films, are considered "slow"; ASA 100 to 200 are in the middle range; and ASA 400 to 1250 and above are "fast" films for use in low light situations. DIN is the European equivalent. Also called exposure index (E.I.), film speed, and speed index.

Aspherical lens. A lens with high speed, sharpness of detail, and relative freedom from aberration.

Astigmatism. Just as in the human eye, astigmatism is a lens defect that makes it impossible to focus both horizontal and vertical lines at the same time. A result of uneven refraction in the lens, astigmatism is closely linked with the *field curvature.* The radius of the sphere formed by the image is determined by the Petzval sum, which is based on the power of the glasses that make up the lens. Astigmatism and curvature of field, like the other aberrations, are corrected by balancing the positive and negative elements in the lens.

Auto converter. See *Tele-extender.*

Automatic diaphragm. Stays open until the shutter is triggered, as opposed to a manual diaphragm, which closes as the lens is stopped down. Automatic diaphragm operation keeps the viewing screen bright in single-lens reflex cameras and makes focusing and metering much easier.

Automatic eye. See *Electronic eye.*

Automatic meter. A built-in exposure meter that reads the amount of light reflected from a subject and automatically adjusts the shutter-speed and/or aperture for an average exposure. Automatic meters take the guesswork out of photography but also prevent the photographer from adjusting for extreme situations or using over- or underexposure for effect.

Autoscreen films. Trademark for an orthochromatic film manufactured by Kodak that produces a screened or dotted image without the use of a special half-tone screen. Autoscreen film is available only in sheets.

Auto-winder. See *Power winder.*

Available light. Any light not purposely set up by the photographer to take the picture. Available light includes indoor as well as outdoor lighting.

Averaging meter. A type of built-in exposure meter that takes a reading from two general areas of the subject and averages them for the final setting. Averaging meters contain two CdS cells to measure the light and then average the readings for the proper exposure. The center-weighted type of averaging meter overlaps the areas read by the cells and becomes, in effect, a combination spot and average meter.

Axis. A theoretical line running directly through the center of the lens elements.

B. Bulb. Included on most shutter speed dials, this setting allows the photographer to hold open the shutter manually for longer time exposures.

Back focus. The distance between the rear of the lens and the focal plane.

Baffle. A shield used on the front of a lens to prevent extraneous light from entering. Baffles are also used around photofloods to direct the light toward the subject and to keep the glare out of the photographer's eyes. One type of baffle is used to cut down on flare in the mirror in a single-lens reflex camera and to cut out unnecessary and extraneous light from a light meter. Also called a lens shade or a sun shade.

Balancing enlarger light. To ensure a pleasing tonal rendition in a color print, the color of the enlarger light must be adjusted. To balance the enlarger light, yellow or magenta filters of varying density are inserted until the light produces the desired tones.

Barrel. The part of a lens that is gripped by the hand. The barrel contains all of the rings that control the lens operation, such as focusing, aperture, and the setting for automatic or manual operation.

Barrel distortion. A lens aberration in which straight lines in the image appear to bow outward. This simple distortion is usually corrected in good lenses; however, some distortion may remain in the glass and is usually only visible at the edges of a picture. Also called positive distortion.

Base. A sheet of gelatin or plastic that holds the light-sensitive emulsion in photographic films. Also called film support.

Base side. The side of the film away from the emulsion.

Baseboard. The bottom support of an enlarger. The baseboard must be large enough to compensate for the height of the enlarger head.

Base-to-base contacting. Placing a negative and a positive with the emulsion sides facing away from each other for a contact print. This method is used to produce line conversions and bas-reliefs.

Bas-relief. A photographic print in which objects appear sculpted from the paper. This illusion is created by a dark shadow line following the contour of one side of the image. Bas-reliefs are produced by off-setting sandwiched positive and negative high-contrast images to create the contour shadow.

Bayonet mount. A type of lens mount. The lens mounts onto the camera and locks into place by lining up a spring-mounted pin with a notched piece of metal on the camera. Because the bayonet also usually serves as the meter-coupling, bayonet mount lenses cannot be automatically stopped down when used with an adapter ring.

BCPS. See *Beam Candlepower Seconds.*

Beam Candlepower Seconds (BCPS). A rating of the amount of light produced by an electronic flash unit.

Behind-the-lens meter. A light meter built into a reflex camera. As the name implies, the meter is located directly behind the lens at the film plane.

Bellows. An expandable, accordion-like attachment used for focusing a lens at a very close range. The bellows is attached between the rear of the lens and the front of the camera to extend the distance of the lens from the focal plane. Because a bellows can be folded in or out, focusing for photomacrographs is much more flexible than when rigid extension rings or tubes are used. Also called multiflex bellows.

Between-the-lens shutter. A type of shutter located between the lens elements. One example of this type of shutter is the leaf shutter.

Blade shutter. See *Leaf shutter.*

Bleaching. Removing the silver image from color film or paper after the three layers of emulsion have been developed. If this silver image is not removed, it will block the colors of the picture. Bleaching is also used to selectively remove silver deposits in black and white prints, in which case it is usually referred to as reducing.

Bleed. Black areas may spread, or bleed, into the white areas in an overexposed high-contrast image. This term can also refer to any image that exceeds its boundaries, such as the edge of a piece of paper.

Bleeder resistor. Part of an electronic flash that allows you to reduce the residual charge by discharging a final flash after the unit is turned off.

Blind. Fits over the eyepiece of a camera to block out unwanted light that can enter the camera through the back and disturb the meter reading.

Blocking up. Overexposing the highlight areas in a photograph. Blocked negatives lack detail in the highlight areas.

Blow up. To enlarge a photograph in order to make a print. Can also refer to the enlargement itself.

Body flange. A metal ring on the front of the camera body that contains the lens mounting system.

Border effect. Increased density at the edge of a high density area next to a low density area in a negative; the opposite of *fringe effect.*

Bounce compensator. A type of electronic eye that can compensate for a bounce flash by taking a reading directly from the subject and adjusting the light output according to the angle of the bounce.

Bounce flash. The flash gun is pointed away from the camera at an angle so that the light can bounce off a wall or the ceiling before striking the subject. Bouncing a flash helps to diffuse light, which is often too harsh.

Box camera. An early camera based on the primitive camera obscura. The box camera looked exactly like a box with a round piece of glass in the front. Kodak promoted amateur photography with a box camera loaded with film that the photographer simply returned, camera and all, to the company's lab for processing. After the film was developed, the camera was returned with a fresh supply of film inside.

Bracketing. To ensure proper exposures, photographers may try several f/stops and shutter speeds on the same subject. This is called bracketing an exposure.

Brightness. The strength or intensity of light or of light areas in a picture.

Broad lighting. Placement of the main light for formal portrait photography. In broad lighting, the light source is placed so that it illuminates the side of the subject's face turned toward the camera. This technique helps to widen thin or narrow faces.

Built-in meter. A light meter encased within the camera that takes a reading of the light reflected from the subject through the camera's viewing system.

Built-in windage. Time allowance for film that is not used promptly. No manufacturer would sell film (either color or black and white) to amateur or part-time photographers that did not have built-in windage, because the storage time in the camera and in the store and the time between shooting and processing are usually much greater than for a professional photographer.

Bulb. A shutter speed setting. See *B*.

Bulk film loader. A large, light-tight plastic case that holds a 100-foot roll of film. Individual cassettes of variable lengths may be loaded from the roll in the bulk film loader.

Bulk film magazine. An attachment that replaces the back of the camera in a mechanized motor drive unit. The bulk film magazine holds enough film for up to 250 exposures and is powered by batteries. This frees the photographer to shoot continuously, if desired, and also allows the camera to be used in scientific and time-lapse photography.

Burn. To expose an image on a film or photographic plate through a negative. A photograph can also be selectively burned to bring up additional detail in highlight areas.

Burning-in. Controlled, prolonged exposure of a precise part of a print. Burning-in is used to bring up detail that may be lost in highlights when exposure is made for shadow detail.

Butterfly lighting. Placement of the main light source in formal portrait photography. In butterfly lighting, the main light source is placed close to the subject so that it casts a shadow underneath the nose. This is said to dramatize glamor pictures of attractive women.

Cable release. A cord, usually 10 inches or longer, that screws into the shutter release. The downward movement of depressing the shutter can jiggle the camera slightly and is especially critical during long exposures. A cable release allows you to trigger the shutter away from the camera to avoid this movement. Most releases have a ring lock for time exposures.

Cadmium sulfide cell. See *CdS cell.*

Calotype. A negative/positive printing process developed by the Englishman William Fox Talbot in the nineteenth century.

Camera body. The case of the camera, which includes all the working parts and the film. The camera body also contains the lens in cameras with set lenses.

Camera obscura. A large, dark room with a small hole in one wall as the light source. Light passing through the pinhole will project an image of the outdoors on the opposite wall. The camera obscura, reduced in size and equipped with a lens, was the forerunner of today's complex cameras.

Candle Meter Second. See *CMS.*

Canned air. Aerosol-packed air in a can. This high-pressure air is used to remove dust and dirt from camera and enlarger lenses and from negatives.

Capacitor. A component in an electronic flash that stores energy. The capacitor builds up energy from a battery (either rechargeable or regular) until it has enough energy stored up to release a flash when the unit is triggered. A ready light lights up on the outside of the flash gun when the capacitor has collected enough energy for another flash.

Cassette. Light-proof casing that holds a roll of film.

CC filters. See *Color compensating filters.*

CdS cell. Cadmium sulfide cell. This light-sensitive cell is used in small hand-held and built-in meters.

Celluloid. Sturdy, flexible plastic that supports the film emulsion. Celluloid was developed in 1887 by a clergyman, who mixed collodion, the emulsion base for wet-plate photography, with camphor and modified the plastic result so that it could be uniformly rolled into very thin sheets.

Center-weighted meter. An averaging meter in which the area sensed by the two CdS cells overlaps. This center part is read twice by both cells and becomes, in effect, a modified *spot meter.*

Chemical fog. An overall dimming of an image as a result of chemical contamination.

Chemical intensifier. See *Intensifier.*

Chromatic aberration. Unequal bending of the various colors of light as they pass through a lens results in an overall fuzziness of the image in black and white photography and in shadows of different colors ringing objects in color photography. This is because the amount of refraction is directly related to the wavelength of the light; for example, blue light, with a shorter wavelength, refracts at a much longer wavelength. Chromatic aberration is divided into two categories, longitudinal and lateral. Lateral chromatic aberration affects the image away from the center, and longitudinal chromatic aberration affects the entire film plane. Both must be corrected for color photography.

-chrome. Suffix used to indicate color slide film. The compound name of the film often includes the company's brand name, such as Kodachrome, Agfachrome, or Fujichrome.

Chromium intensifier. A chemical used to build up the silver image on film. Also referred to as intensifier.

Cibachrome. A color printing method that makes a print directly from a color slide. This method is noted for its clarity and brilliance of color, which are due to the absence of the usual *inter-negative* used to print from a slide.

Circular polarizer. A specially designed polarizing filter for use with single-lens reflex cameras that have built-in polarized metering.

Cliché-verre. A photographic print made from a drawing on a transparent or translucent base instead of the normal negative.

Clip-on meter. An auxiliary light meter that can be attached directly to the outside of the camera body.

Close-up lens. A lens used to focus closer to an object than normal. *Macro lenses* are one type of close-up lens.

CMS. Stands for Candle Meter Seconds. A basic unit of light measure that is derived from the exposure of sensitive material for one second to a light source of one candle power at one meter.

Coated lens. A lens with a chemically treated surface to reduce internal reflection of light between the glass-to-air surfaces of the elements. Coating, by reducing reflection, increases the amount of image-producing light that reaches the film surface. The internal reflection of light is also called flare. Also called a multicoated lens.

Cold tone paper. Photographic paper with a blue cast to the blacks and grays produced. Cold tone paper also has a very brilliant white background.

-color. A suffix used to indicate color print film. As in color slide film, the film name is usually a composite of the company name and the suffix, such as Kodacolor, Fujicolor, or Agfacolor.

Color balance. Film is sensitized, or balanced, to produce colors that we perceive as "normal." Since not all light will produce the same colors, color film is balanced for either daylight or tungsten. However, not all lighting situations provide the same type of light as the color balance of the film, and unnatural shades will result unless special filters are used to compensate for this lack of balance.

Color compensating filters. Filters used to correct color balance in film. Color compensating filters may be used to correct the color balance of daylight film so that it may be used indoors and to correct tungsten film to produce more normal results outdoors. Adjustments for different colors of light, such as fluorescent, are also made with color compensating filters. Also called CC filters.

Color contrast. The visible difference between colors that is translated into gray tones in black and white photography.

Color control patches. Standardized color comparison scales used to achieve faithful reproduction of color when copying artwork. The scales are marked in 9 patches of standard colors and 10 patches of tones ranging from pure white to solid black.

Color film processing. See *Subtractive process.*

Color filters. Glass disks placed in front of the camera lens to achieve different tones. In black and white photography, these filters can change the range of grays. For instance, by using a red filter, you can render the sky almost black. Filters are also used in color photography to compensate for unbalanced light.

Color formers. See *Coupler compounds.*

Color head. A specially designed enlarger head, which contains all the filters necessary for color printing. A color head can be extremely complicated and is sometimes computerized for exact filtration.

Color-Key. Trademark for a pigmented photosensitive emulsion on a plastic base. When exposed to ultraviolet light, Color-Key produces a colored image. Manufactured by 3M, Color-Key is usually used for color proofing in the graphic arts industry but can also be used to produce striking colors in color printing.

Color printing filters. See *CP filters.*

Color rendition chart. A card containing standard color tones. It can be used to check the color reproductive capabilities of a film type or of a projector. A photograph of the card held by a model is developed for the flesh tones. The resulting picture or slide can then be compared directly with the color rendition chart to verify the actual tonal rendition.

Color-reversal film. Film used to create color transparencies or slides. Instead of forming a negative color image, color reversal film forms a positive image in the colors expected by the eye.

Color saturation. Strengthened color in a negative or slide produced by slightly underexposing the film.

Color temperature. The balance of colors in a light source. This balance is measured by temperature in degrees Kelvin, an absolute temperature scale. Color temperature may be a misleading factor, because two sources could emit light at the same temperature and have a slightly different distribution of color. This effect can be seen in comparing daylight to a light source with the same approximate temperature, such as a fluorescent lamp. Photographs taken with daylight film under fluorescent lighting will be noticeably green.

Color temperature meter. An instrument used to measure the *color balance* of a light source.

Color translation. Reproduction of colors as gray tones in black and white photography.

Color transparency. A photograph on color reversal film, usually called a slide.

Coma. A defect in a lens that shows as a comet-shaped blurring of part of the image away from the center of the film. When light passes through the lens at an oblique angle, not all the rays focus at the same spot. This produces a sharp, luminous point with a tail of diffuse light. Coma aberration, which increases in size as the angle of light becomes more extreme, is corrected by pairing concave and convex lenses and may also be partially controlled by the lens aperture. At the larger openings, coma aberration is compounded by another aberration, *astigmatism,* producing much more complicated light patches.

Come up. Common parlance used to describe how an image develops in a darkroom. After exposure, a seemingly blank sheet begins to show a faint image soon after being plunged into developer. The print is left in the developer until the image builds up (or comes up) to its fullest extent.

Composite negative. A single negative made from several high-contrast positive separations. Composite negatives are used to produce posterized images and contain all the intermediate tonal values of the posterized image.

Composition. The pleasing arrangement of objects, lines, textures, or colors in a picture.

Compound lens. One that consists of two or more optical elements, which are sometimes cemented together.

Condenser. (1) A large piece of glass located between the light source and lens in an enlarger. The condenser directs and concentrates the light for stronger projection. (2) The *capacitor* in an electronic flash.

Contact print. A print made by placing a negative directly on photographic paper for the exposure. Since there is no enlargement, the print is the same size as the negative.

Contact printing frame. A hinged piece of glass with a negative holding strip for making contact prints or contact sheets. The negative or strips of negatives are placed between the glass and the paper and held in place securely for the length of exposure.

Contact sheet. A contact print made of an entire roll of film on one piece of paper. Contact sheets make it easier for the photographer to view each negative for content and clarity before printing. Also called a proof sheet.

Contacting. Placing a negative directly on another piece of film or paper for exposure.

Continuous-tone development. Chemical processing of orthochromatic and panchromatic films. Continuous-tone development yields negatives with a wide range of gray tones, as opposed to high-contrast and lith development.

Continuous-tone negative. A black and white negative with a wide range of gray tones.

Continuously variable focal length lens. A rather wordy but descriptive term for a *Zoom lens.*

Contour sharpness. See *Acutance.*

Contrast. The tonal range between light and dark in a photograph. In a photograph with high contrast, many of the middle gray tones have been lost—either in exposure, developing, or printing.

Contrast filters. Used to increase or decrease tonal separation in black and white photography.

Contrast gradient. The measure of the extent of contrast or separation of gray tones in a print or negative.

Contrast index. A constant coefficient used to determine the proper developing times for different films.

Convertible lens. A type of double lens that may be used as separate elements for a greater focal length. The front and rear elements are designed so that they can be used either together or separately.

Copy negative. A negative made from a print or flat artwork for reproduction or enlargement. Since pictures from Polaroid and other "instant" cameras have no usable negative, a copy negative must be made for duplicate prints. Copy negatives are also made for large orders of one photograph. The large contact negative can be quickly and easily contact-printed for thousands of pictures.

Correction filters. Used to change gray tones to correspond to the expected color values and to correct for the uneven sensitivity to colors of some film emulsions.

Coupled range-finder. A focusing system used in a rangefinder camera. The focusing mechanism in the lens is connected to the range-finder, which contains a split image for focusing. As the image is lined up in the range-finder, the lens is also brought into focus. Also called range-finder focusing system or range-finder.

Coupler compounds. Chemicals present in color film and paper emulsions, which when combined with developer, produce the dyes that make up the colored image. Also called color formers.

Coupling ring. The part of the lens that attaches to the camera and connects the lens mechanism with the shutter and meter. This coupling is important because most lenses *stop down* automatically when you shoot the picture.

Covering power. The ability of a lens to create an image of good quality throughout the film plane.

CP filters. Color printing filters. These are acetate filters used to produce a pleasing color balance in a color print. The filters are in varying densities of three colors: an ultraviolet absorbing filter, magenta, and yellow. Different combinations of as many filters as necessary are placed in the filter drawer of the enlarger. This group of filters used together for printing is called the filter pack.

Cronalith. Trademark for DuPont's lith film and developer.

Cropping. Removing unwanted portions of a picture in the enlarging. The easel is placed so that these portions are excluded, and the enlarger is adjusted so that only the part of the picture desired appears within the easel frame.

Curtain shutter. See *Focal plane shutter.*

Curvature of field. This aberration is caused by light passing through the lens directly on the axis and forming an image closer to the lens than light passing through the lens at an angle. The result is an image formed on a curved surface, not plane. When not properly corrected, curvature of the field is responsible for loss of resolution at the edges of the film plane. Also called field curvature. See also *Astigmatism.*

Curvilinear distortion. See *Distortion.*

Cut film. See *Sheet film.*

Cyan. The blue primary that is part of the basis of color printing and slides. The other two primaries are magenta (red) and yellow.

Cylindrical perspective. A distortion of perspective created by a camera whose lens swings in an arc during the exposure to cover a wider range. As a result of the swing, straight lines running in the direction of the swing tend to bow outward at the center and run together at the edges. Straight lines running perpendicular to the swing are reproduced as straight.

D-8. Trademark for a high-contrast film developer manufactured by Kodak.

D-11. Trademark for a high-contrast film developer manufactured by Kodak.

D-19. Trademark for a high-contrast film developer manufactured by Kodak.

D-76. Trademark for a popular film developer manufactured by Kodak.

Daguerreotype. An early photographic form developed by the Frenchman Louis Daguerre. Daguerreotypes are sensitized, silver-coated metal plates, which are exposed to light in a camera, then developed with mercury vapor. The image formed is a bright, shiny alloy of the mercury and silver.

Darkroom. A room that can be completely sealed off from

all light for photographic development.

Darkroom cloth. Light-proof heavy black cloth used to keep light out of a darkroom.

Daze. To overpower with light; to strike with too strong lustre; to hinder the act of seeing by too much light suddenly introduced.

Definition. Overall sharpness of an image produced by a lens. Definition is impaired by lens aberrations and may be improved in most instances by stopping down the lens.

Dektol. A chemical used to develop photographic prints.

Dense negative. One that has a heavy build-up of silver particles. Because of its thickness, a dense negative is hard to print properly.

Densitometer. A photometer designed to measure the density of a negative for printing. Most densitometers have three parts: a photocell encased in a hand-held sensor; an ammeter to record the difference in densities; and a light source—usually an enlarger. The negative is projected on the easel, and the photocell is placed in what appears to be the densest part of the projected image. A reading may be obtained from the ammeter, which is adjusted for the paper type, and a test is made. A densitometer helps to guarantee a good exposure with maximum shadow detail and is used to cut time and guesswork in the darkroom.

Density. A measure of the ability of a negative to transmit light. Light does not pass as readily through the negative where there is a greater build-up of metallic silver. This build-up, which is a direct result of the exposure and development of the film, determines many aspects of the final print, such as contrast and detail.

Depth of field. The zone of sharpness just in front and

behind the point of focus. Depth of field varies with the distance from the subject, focal length of the lens, and aperture. The greater the focal length and larger the aperture, the shallower the depth of field will be. This factor is especially critical when taking portraits with a long lens such as a 105 mm. Sometimes, in low light situations, the depth can be so shallow that if you focus on a person's nose, their eyes or ears will be out of focus. Most lenses have a scale below the focusing ring to indicate depth of field at a particular distance and f/stop.

Depth of field scale. A series of lines and numbers, usually just below the focusing ring of a lens, that indicates depth of field at a particular distance and f/stop.

Depth of focus. Similar to depth of field, depth of focus is the critical area that can be considered in focus in a photograph. Arrived at through an elaborate set of formulae, depth of focus determines the amount of room for error that is allowed for the focusing screen and the film plane in a camera.

Deutsche Industrie Norm. See *DIN*.

Develop by inspection. An emergency procedure used when you suspect that the film was improperly exposed. By inspecting the film quickly under controlled conditions, you can determine whether to extend development or to switch the film to a specialized developer.

Developable image. That part of a film's emulsion which, after exposure, has the capability of producing a visible image after development with the proper chemicals. Also called latent image.

Developer. Chemical used to produce an image on exposed paper or film.

Developer exhaustion. Whether for film or paper, developer can only convert so many silver compounds to silver before wearing out. As the developer wears out, or is exhausted, it will change from clear to yellowish, and finally to brown. As this is happening, development will take longer, and eventually quality will begin to deteriorate rapidly. In addition, developer can be exhausted chemically by contamination from either stop-bath or fixer. Light breaks down developer, so it should always be stored in dark bottles.

Developer streaks. A chemical distortion of a film image caused by insufficient agitation during development. The image develops unevenly (in streaks) because some of the film surfaces are not being exposed to fresh developer.

Developing agent. The ingredient in developer that chemically frees metallic silver from the light-struck crystals in the emulsion. This metallic silver is deposited on the film base to form the image.

Diaphragm. Overlapping metal leaves located inside the lens, which control the size of the aperture. The diaphragm may be made larger or smaller by adjusting the f/stops.

Diaphragm star. A pattern caused by a pinpoint bright light source photographed at a very small aperture.

Diazo process. A dry color printing process that produces a positive image from a positive image. Diazo prints are of only one color plus white and are used largely for making blueprints and duplicating microfilm.

Dichroic filter. A type of plastic filter used to balance the light for color printing.

Diffraction. The spreading of light around the edges of an object. Diffraction increases as the aperture is decreased and is only a problem when the lens is stopped down so far that the disc formed by the diffracted light becomes visible in an enlargement. Manufacturers of lenses control the distortion by limiting the f/stops of the lens in relation to the size film used. As a result, in most lenses used with 35 mm cameras, there are no apertures smaller than f/16.

Diffuser. Anything used to soften or reduce the amount of light passing through a camera, enlarger lens, or light meter. In old, romantic movies, the cameraman would always slip an old nylon stocking over the lens of the camera before shooting the heroine so that she would appear slightly softer and a bit more diaphanous in contrast to her male lead. A diffuser must be translucent and not so thick as to absorb too much light.

Diffuser filter. Pieces of glass placed in front of either a camera or an enlarger lens to diffuse the light. They are called filters only because they have the same type of mounting as regular filters. Diffuser filters have finely etched lines or dots to scatter the light for a softening effect.

Diffuser plate. A sheet of cloudy or frosted glass placed between the light source and the negative carrier in an enlarger. The diffuser plate softens the light, spreads it evenly over the projection surface, and eliminates excessive contrast.

Diffusion screen. A piece of cloudy or finely lined glass placed in front of the camera's lens to soften outlines in a portrait.

Diffusion-transfer-reversal. See *DTR*.

Diminution. The decrease in size of an object as it moves away from the camera. This type of perspective creates a sense of depth because the human eye is used to certain size relationships.

DIN. Deutsche Industrie Norm. This is the European equivalent of *ASA*. Instead of the arithmetic principle used for ASA, DIN is a numerical rating based on a logarithmic scale.

Diode. A semiconductor that can either emit or transmit energy. Diodes are used in cameras to measure the amount of light reflected from an object (GAP or silicon blue cells are used in a light meter) or to indicate the proper exposure in the view finder (LEDs, which glow according to the proper setting, are used).

Direct development. The process that produces a silver image from exposed silver halides.

Dispersion. The difference in the refraction of light of various wavelengths. The dispersion of a piece of glass may be measured by determining the refractive index of the light.

Dispersive power. The ability of a lens to refract light of different wavelengths. The dispersive power of a lens is usually expressed in Abbe numbers, which are arrived at by determining the relationship between the angles of refraction and deviation of a lens.

Dissolve control. A feature on some slide projectors that permits synchronized fading from one image into another from a second projector.

Distance scale. Lines and numbers on the focusing ring that indicate how far the camera is from the subject. Electronic flash guns also have a distance scale to help determine what f/stop to use for the amount of flash. These distance scales are connected to the ASA setting.

Distortion. Bending of straight lines of an image. Also called curvilinear distortion. Distortion varies with magnification and the distance of the object from the axis of the lens. (1) The two types of distortion classified as aberrations are negative, or pincushion, distortion, where the vertical lines tend to bend inward, and positive, or barrel, distortion, where the straight lines of the image bow outward. This simple distortion is easily corrected in a multiple element lens of normal focal length. (2) Another type of distortion occurs with the increased magnification of telephoto lenses and the wider viewing range of wide-angle lenses. In both cases, the perspective is visibly distorted. This type of distortion cannot be completely corrected but can be taken into account when shooting a picture with either type of lens.

DK-60a. Trademark for a rapid developer manufactured by Kodak.

Dodging. A method used in printing to protect parts of a picture from overexposure.

Dot screen tint. A dotted patterned screen used to modify the tones of a photographic print.

Double condenser. A type of optical system used in an enlarger. A double condenser consists of two large convex lenses, which collect and concentrate the light through the negative.

Double exposure. A frame of film that has been exposed twice, to two different subjects. The double exposure appears as a layered image of the two scenes.

Double weight. See *DW*.

Dry-cell unit. An electronic flash that is powered by a large 510-volt battery.

Dry mounting. Adhering a photograph, drawing, map, or other thin sheet of paper on a stiff backing without using wet glue. The most popular form of dry mounting used for photographs utilizes a heated press and double-waxed mounting tissue. Tissue is placed between the photograph and the board, and this sandwich is placed under pressure and heat in a dry mounting press for a predetermined interval—usually about one minute. The photograph is then permanently mounted on the backing.

Dry mounting tissue. Double-waxed paper, which when heated, adheres a photograph to a stiff surface such as cardboard or heavy mounting board.

DTR. Diffusion-transfer-reversal. This process is used to produce a direct positive print and forms the basis for Polaroid and other "instant camera" film.

Dupe. Slang term used for a duplicate slide.

Duplicate negative. An exact replica of a negative made by contact printing the negative on another piece of film.

DW. Stands for Double Weight. This is an extra heavy printing paper used when the photograph is either very large or not intended for mounting.

Dye colors. Produced in color film by the combination of developer and special coupler compounds, these dye colors—yellow, magenta, and cyan—combine to reproduce most colors in color films and paper.

Dye couplers. See *Coupler compounds.*

Dye density. The thickness of the dye layer formed in the film by the coupler compounds is directly related to the density of the silver image that is first formed by the developer. The dye density then determines the intensity of the color in the resulting picture; for slides, a greater dye density produces greater color saturation, while for color prints, the converse is true.

Dye transfer process. A method of color printing in which the image is transferred from film to paper. In the dye transfer process, three color separations of the positive image are used to make the print. The value of this process is that the color balance can be much more precisely controlled, since the color of the image is reproduced and broken down into three separate images. Also called inhibition process.

Easel. Device used to hold printing paper flat under an enlarger during projection.

Easel distortion. This occurs when the easel holding the enlarging paper is not level with the plane of the negative. Easel distortion is often used intentionally to give the impression of movement to an otherwise flat photograph.

ECPS. See *Effective Candlepower Seconds.*

EE. See *Electronic eye.*

Effective Candlepower Seconds (ECPS). A   measurement of the light produced by an electronic flash unit.

EH. Trademark for daylight-type high-speed Ektachrome color slide film manufactured by Kodak.

EHB. Trademark for tungsten-type high-speed Ektachrome color slide film manufactured by Kodak.

E.I. Exposure Index. This is usually referred to as *ASA.*

18-percent reflectance gray card. This is the full name of a handy accessory often called simply a gray card, *gray scale,* or neutral gray card. A gray card is exactly that—a piece of cardboard that is of a uniform, middle tone of gray. In confusing lighting situations, a meter reading can be taken directly from the gray card, which is placed so that the light reflects off it. A good substitute for the gray card is the palm of the hand, held well away from the meter.

Ektamatic paper. Trademark for Kodak's *Stabilization paper.*

Ektamatic processor. Trademark for Kodak's *Stabilization processor.*

Electromagnetic spectrum. The range of radiant energy,

measured in wavelengths, that includes visible light, ultra-violet, and infrared as well as x-rays, gamma rays, and radio waves.

Electronic eye (EE). A sensor built into an electronic flash gun that reads the amount of light present and regulates the intensity of the flash accordingly. Unless the flash is used in total darkness, the electronic eye always conserves part of the stored energy in the *capacitor*. This results in a less harsh and bright flash and saves the charge in the battery so that the flash does not need recharging or new batteries quite as often. Also called an automatic eye.

Electronic flash. An auxiliary light source that emits a split-second brilliant white light. The electronic flash uses energy stored in a *capacitor* from either batteries or regular household current to ignite a small quantity of gas inside a glass tube. The mixture of gases, such as krypton and xenon, glows brightly, producing a brief burst of light that may be used to stop fast action. Because of this charac-teristic, electronic flashes are also called speedlights and strobes. Also called a flash gun.

Electrophotography. A method used to produce an image using electrostatic charges instead of chemicals. This is the basis of photocopying machines.

Emulsion. The mixture of chemicals and compounds that react with light to produce an image on film or paper.

Emulsion-to-emulsion contacting. Reproducing a negative by contacting it on another piece of film. Both emulsions must be touching to ensure sharpness and detail in the copy.

Enlarger. The most basic piece of darkroom equipment. Enlargers project light through a negative onto a flat easel, which holds photographic paper. The quality of the finished product can be determined by many factors, including the type of light source used, the type of condensing or diffusing system, and the optical quality of the enlarging lens. The basic parts of an enlarger are the head, which holds the light source, condenser and/or diffuser, the filter drawer, the negative carrier, the bellows, the lens and diaphragm, and the focusing control; the supporting column with a counterweight to balance the enlarger head; and the baseboard. Also called a projection printer.

Enlarger foot-switch. This handy device allows you to trigger the enlarger light source and timer with your foot instead of manually, leaving your hands free to make other adjustments.

Enlarger head. Contains most of the working parts of an enlarger. Included in the enlarger head are the light source, the condenser and/or diffuser, the filter drawer, the negative holder, the bellows, the lens and diaphragm, and the focusing control.

Enlarger timer. An electrical control that limits the length of time that the enlarger light is lit. The timer connects to the enlarger through the electrical system and usually has markings for time periods from 1 to 60 seconds.

Enlarging paper. Paper cut to standard sizes and coated with a light-sensitive emulsion for printing photographs. Enlarging paper (also called printing paper, photographic paper, or simply paper) is available in single or double weight and with a wide variety of both paper stocks and emulsions. Ordinary black and white printing paper is graded from zero to 6 according to its ability to record gray tones. The zero grade, which is a soft or low-contrast paper, is used with a negative that has too high a contrast. The 6 paper is considered a very high contrast paper and produces few gray tones. Most negatives reproduce in solid black and white on such a hard, or high contrast, paper.

Enlarging paper is also available with a variable contrast emulsion. This emulsion can be softened or hardened by using special filters in the enlarger. Enlarging paper may have a matte surface, flat finished surface, or a high gloss surface, in addition to several special textured finishes such as silk, rough, and fabric. Enlarging paper is also produced in warm or cold tones; this refers to the paper stock, which can be anything from a harsh cold blue-white to a much warmer cream color. Novelty papers are made by several companies with paper stocks of bright blues, red, yellow, and other colors. Colored prints may also be achieved by using a chemical paper toner, which dyes the paper different colors.

EPD. Trademark for Kodak's E-6 daylight-type Ekta-chrome color slide film, rated at 200 ASA.

EPT. Trademark for Kodak's tungsten-type E-6 Ekta-chrome color slide film, rated at 160 ASA.

Estar. A type of plastic film base.

Ex. factor. Part of the white light data of color printing paper. The Ex. factor indicates the sensitivity to light of a particular batch of printing paper and is used as a guide for adjusting the exposure time.

Expiration date. The limit of a film's dependable color reproduction. This is always printed on the film box and indicates the point at which the color balance will begin to seriously deteriorate.

Exposure. The length of time that light is allowed to strike the film or paper to produce an image.

Exposure Index (E.I.). See *ASA*.

Exposure latitude. The range of the amount of light neces-sary to produce an acceptable image on film. As a rule, black and white films are less sensitive than color films to slight under- or overexposure and thus are said to have a wider ex-posure latitude.

Exposure meter. See *Light meter.*

Extender. See *Tele-extender.*

Extension ring. See *Extension tube.*

Extension tube. A set of rigid tubes that fit between the camera body and lens. Extension tubes are used in close-up or macrophotography to magnify the subject for life-size or larger than life-size pictures. Also called extension ring.

Eye-level view-finder. One that is used by holding it up to the eye. Most single-lens reflex cameras use eye-level view-finders exclusively.

Eyepiece. A piece of glass fitted into the rear of the camera for viewing the subject through the lens of a single-lens reflex camera.

f/number. See *f/stop.*

f/stop. Number engraved on the lens indicating the relative aperture. This is computed by dividing the focal length of the lens by the diameter of the diaphragm opening. The lowest number found on a particular lens—such as f/2—indicates the maximum light transmission capability of the lens. Lower, wider apertures also restrict the depth of field and depth of focus, thereby limiting the overall clarity of the picture. Also called f/number, lens opening, or relative aperture.

Factorial development. Exact timing of the development of a print for optimum reproduction and development of the emulsion.

Fall-off. Lack of crisp image at the edge of a print as a result of various lens aberrations.

Farmer's reducer. Kodak's trademark for packaged potassium ferricyanide and fixer. Farmer's reducer is used to rescue the metallic silver in prints and film.

Field. The area covered by a lens, excluding the axis.

Field curvature. See *Curvature of field.*

Fill-in light. Secondary light used in portrait photography and other studio shots to give added detail and highlight to the side of the face or object away from the main light. A small electronic flash is sometimes used to fill in detail in outdoor portraits when the sun is behind the subject.

Film advance. The lever located at the top right of most single-lens reflex cameras. This lever turns the take-up spool inside the camera and advances the film one frame at a time.

Film pack. A light-proof box containing a number of sheets of film ready for exposure. Protective paper with tabs lies between each sheet to shield it from light during an exposure. Polaroid Land cameras used film packs.

Film plane. The flat frame of film located directly behind the lens of a camera. During exposure, this film plane reacts to light passing through the lens. The light from the lens focuses on the film, or focal plane.

Film processing. The chemical method used to produce an image on film.

Film registration. Alignment of positive or negative images on different pieces of film. Registration is critical in making negatives for special effects such as posterization, sandwiching, and photo-silk-screen processes.

Film speed. See *ASA.*

Film support. See *Base.*

Film transport. The mechanism that carries the film across the focal plane in a camera.

Filter. A colored piece of glass or acetate used to block various wavelengths of light. When used in front of a lens, filters are made of glass. These pieces of glass absorb light of the same wavelengths as the color of the filter and cut down on the amount of light reaching the film. In addition to affecting exposure, filters also affect the tonal balance in black and white and the color balance in color photography. For instance, in black and white photography, a red filter drastically alters the gray tones in an outdoor photograph by creating an almost black sky with bright white clouds.

In color photography, the same red filter gives an even red cast to the entire picture. Filters used for color photography usually are not any one strong color. Instead, they are specially balanced to correct the color of light in certain situations such as candlelight or fluorescent light and to correct the balance of a color film.

Other types of filters are *polarizing filters, acetate filters,* and *diffuser filters.*

Filter drawer. A compartment located in the enlarger head between the lamp and the negative. The drawer holds color compensating filters for color printing or variable contrast filters used in black and white printing.

Filter factor. Because most filters absorb light to a lesser or greater degree, the exposure must be adjusted for the density of the filter. The amount of adjustment that must be made is called the filter factor. As a rule, proportionately more light is absorbed as the wavelength increases, making red the densest of the color filters. Filter factors cannot be computed for specialty filters such as those used in infrared photography, since these filters absorb *all* visible light to allow free transmission of the infrared rays.

Filter holder. Enlargers not equipped with a filter drawer have a ring mounted beneath the lens. This holder accommodates a gelatin-type filter for use with both variable contrast and color printing papers.

Filter pack. The collection of filters assembled to balance the enlarger light. A filter pack can contain from two to as many color correcting or compensating filters as you own. See under *CP filters*.

Fine-grain developer. A chemical used to improve the grain of film by development. Unfortunately, fine-grain developers, such as Kodak's Microdol-X, Ilford's Microphen, and Edwal's Super 20, also tend to cut down on contrast and film speed.

Fish-eye lens. An ultra–wide-angle lens that encompasses a 180 degree viewing field.

Five-pod. A five-legged stand used to provide more rigid support for a camera and long lens than is possible with the usual three-legged stand, or tripod.

5247. A fine-grain, ASA 100 color movie-film that is sometimes packed in 35mm rolls of 20 and 36 exposures for still photography. The advantage of this type of movie film is that good, clear contact positives are made at the time of development, yielding both negatives for prints and positives for slides from the same roll of film.

Fixed focus. A type of lens that focuses only at a certain point. Fixed focus is offered in many longer lenses to drastically reduce the price; however, it also considerably reduces the versatility of a lens.

Fixed mirror. Unlike a single-lens reflex camera, in which the mirror must flip up out of the way while the film is exposed, a twin-lens reflex camera is equipped with an immovable, fixed mirror behind the lens used for focusing and viewing. The other lens in the camera contains the aperture and directs the light to the film plane for the exposure.

Fixer. Sodium thiosulfate, the chemical used to stop the reaction of light with the silver particles on film or paper. Often referred to as *hypo.*

Fixer exhaustion. Just as in developer exhaustion, fixer eventually wears out. Exhaustion is speeded up by exposure to light and high temperatures, contamination from developer or other chemicals, and excessive use.

Flare. Light that is scattered through internal reflection (another name for flare) in a lens. This light reaches the film as a sort of fog and will not produce an image. This fog can reduce shadow contrast and may also produce light spots in the image. One of the most common renderings of flare can be seen when a photographer shoots directly into a strong light source such as the sun. The sun is reproduced in the picture as several patches of light in the shape of the lens diaphragm. Flare is corrected by coating the lens elements in order to retard reflection.

Flash bulb. Used as supplemental illumination, flash bulbs emit a bright light when triggered by the camera's shutter. Bulbs come in many sizes and are mounted in front of a reflector so that the light can be directed toward the subject. Also called a photoflash lamp.

Flash gun. See *Electronic flash.*

Flash ring. A circular electronic flash used for close-up photography. Because most flash guns are mounted either on top of the camera or to the side, they often do not illuminate the field in extreme closeups. A flash ring, which fits around the camera's lens, is used instead to illuminate a small field directly in front of the lens. Also called a ring light.

Flash synchronization. A timing device built into a camera to trigger the flash and shutter simultaneously. A PC connector cord is often used to make a connection between an auxiliary flash unit and the camera.

Flash terminals. Connections installed in a camera for synchronizing the flash with the shutter.

Flashcube. A four-sided flash unit containing separate filaments. Each filament is backed with a small reflector inside the cube, which mounts directly on top of the camera. Flashcubes are generally used only on small, simple cameras such as Kodak Instamatics or the nonsophisticated types of Polaroid Land cameras.

Flashing. Re-exposing a photographic print to white light while it is in the developer. Flashing produces a type of solarized image as a result of the *Sabattier effect.*

Flood light. A bright light used in studio work. Flood lights may be directed toward the subject by using a reflector behind the light. The distance from the lamp to the reflector determines the size of the beam that will hit the subject.

Focal length. The distance from the exact center of a lens to the point at which the light focuses. Measured in millimeters, centimeters, or inches, the focal length of a lens is directly proportional to the magnification of the image. Standard lenses for 35 mm cameras range from 45 to 55 mm. Telephoto lenses, such as 135 or 200 mm, create the illusion of bringing the subject closer to the camera, while wide-angle lenses (28 or 17 mm) take in a larger area than normally seen by the eye and tend to distort the image.

Focal plane. As rays of light pass through the camera's lens, they are brought to a focus and form an image on the film, which forms a flat surface. This flat surface acts as the focal plane, or plane of focus, for the lens.

Focal plane shutter. A thin curtain that passes across the film surface at variable speeds to control exposure. This type of shutter is located just in front of the focal plane and derives its name from its position. Also called a curtain shutter.

Focal point. The point of focus of a lens. A collection of focal points from light passing through the lens forms the *focal plane.*

Focus. The point at which light beams converge after passing through a lens. To the human eye, this is also the point of most clarity of an image.

Focusing magnifier. An aid used for critical fine focusing on a viewfinder.

Focusing scale. A series of lines and numbers, usually in both feet and meters, used to determine the proper focus for a distance from a subject.

Focusing screen. See *Viewing screen.*

Focusing system. The mechanism in a camera designed to bring an image into focus. The focusing system in most cameras moves the lens elements until the image is clear on the ground glass viewing screen. This adjustment is done with a ring on the lens barrel. Early cameras moved the entire lens back and forth with a bellows.

Fog. The overall tone that appears on film or paper after accidental brief exposure to light.

Foot-candle. The most commonly used photometric measure in photography. The foot-candle is equal to the direct illumination of a surface in a one-foot range from a light source of one standard candle.

Foreshortening distortion. An optical problem of wide-angle lenses. Because of a wider viewing angle than the human eye, these lenses distort the normal perspective proportions. Objects close to the camera appear abnormally large, while items a little bit farther away seem disproportionately small.

Formalin fixer. A chemical used in color processing to prevent images on film and paper from fading prematurely.

Forming. Educating your electronic flash capacitor to accept a full charge. Forming is carried out by gradually charging and discharging the flash gun according to the manufacturer's directions.

Formolith. Trademark for Ilford's lith film and developer.

Frame. The area of film exposed by the shutter during an exposure. The frame of film forms the *focal plane* of the lens.

Freeze. To stop motion abruptly.

Fresnel lens. A flat sheet of plastic scored with concentric lines. The fresnel lens is placed directly under the camera's viewing screen to help illuminate the entire viewing area of a single-lens reflex camera.

Fringe effect. Decreased density at the edge of a low density area next to an area of high density in a negative; the opposite of *border effect.*

Full-aperture metering. A very smart built-in light meter automatically adjusts its reaction to light as you stop down the lens; however, the aperture of the lens remains fully open to allow the maximum amount of light for viewing. The aperture closes only when the shutter is released. This process is called full-aperture metering.

Fully automatic. A term denoting an automatic camera that selects shutter speed for you.

Fully automatic diaphragm. In this type of camera design, the diaphragm stays wide open during focusing, reading of the meter, and other operations, and automatically closes down to the preselected stop when the shutter is released.

Gallium arsenic phosphorus photo diode. A light-sensitive diode used to measure light reflected from an object through the lens of a camera. This type of light meter, also called a GAP cell, reacts faster than the CdS type and does not require the infrared filtration that the silicon blue cell seems to need.

Gamma. A mathematical designation used by manufacturers to determine the various conditions for development, such as length, temperature of solution, type of solution, and agitation.

GAP cell. See *Gallium arsenic phosphorus photo diode.*

Gevalith. Trademark for Agfa-Gevaert's lith film and developer.

Ghost images. Vague outlines sometimes seen in photographs. These images are often caused by excess light reflected off the film backing.

Gilding. A type of reversal effect that is the result of preexposure and longer development of Polaroid film.

Glacial acetic acid. Chemical used to abruptly stop development of film or paper. This is usually called *stop-bath.*

Glassines. Semitransparent envelopes used to protect negatives and slides from dust and other contaminants.

Glossy surface. Bright, shiny surface on photographic paper. Glossiness is created by hardening the surface of the paper with chemicals and heat.

Glow light. See *Ready light.*

Gold sensitizing. An increase in the ability of a film's emulsion to react to light as a result of added salts of gold.

Graduate. A measuring container used in the darkroom for mixing chemicals.

Grain. The visible particles of silver that make up an image. The size of the particles determines the graininess of a print or type of film.

Granularity. The graininess, or size of grains, in a particular film or print.

Graphic arts developer. See *Lith developer.*

Graphic arts film. See *Lith film.*

Gray scale. (1) A card containing a series of gray tones from white to black. This card is used to determine faithfulness of color and tone in photographic reproductions. Also called a gray card, 18-percent reflectance gray card, or neutral gray card. (2) A gray scale is also the basis for Ansel Adams's *zone system* used to determine proper exposure of pictures. Also called a tonal scale.

Great Yellow Father. A fond, tongue-in-cheek nickname for the Kodak Company.

Gremlins. Evil spirits that sometimes occupy darkrooms and cameras, causing rack and ruin of pictures. Gremlins, which are responsible for most of the dirt and dust appearing on prints, can be controlled by scrupulously caring for equipment and taking all precautions with film and paper.

Ground glass. Translucent glass used to focus the image in a camera. The ground glass makes up the viewing screen and is used interchangeably with that term.

Guide number. Numerical guide used with flash equipment to determine distance and f/stop. The guide number varies for each film and type of flash.

Gum bichromate emulsion. An antiquated method of photographic printing. This process is being revived because of its adaptation to graphic reproduction and color. The gum bichromate emulsion may be colored with watercolor paints to produce two-tone images. Because of a distinct lack of speed, most applications of this process are limited.

Hairlight. A light used to illuminate the outline of the hair at the crown of the head in portrait photography. Also called a top light.

Halation. An effect caused by light reflecting from the film base back through the emulsion. This phenomenon is controlled by an antihalation backing used in all modern film. Without this backing, the image would have halos around the bright spots from the reflected light.

Halftone. A photograph reproduced on lith film. The gray areas of the photograph are represented by dots of varying sizes. Halftones are used in offset and silk-screen printing to reproduce photographs.

Hand-held meter. A light meter used independently of the camera and held in the hand for operation.

Hard paper. Printing paper with very high contrast.

Hardener. A chemical, usually potassium alum, added to fixer to prevent the film emulsion from softening or swelling during washing.

Haze filter. See *UV filter.*

Head shot. A photograph of a person in which the head comprises most of the frame.

Helical-focusing lens. One in which the mechanism for focusing the lens moves the elements further from or closer to the focal plane by means of a spiral mechanism. Enlargers often have helical-focusing lenses.

Hemispherical diffuser. Used on hand-held meters to change the reading from reflected to incident light. A hemispherical diffuser also increases the angle of acceptance to a full 180 degrees to measure all the light coming toward the subject. Colloquially known as a spherical diffuser.

High contrast. A print or negative with little or no tonal separation. High-contrast images are almost completely rendered in blacks and whites and lack a great deal of detail. However, when handled with good taste and judgment, high-contrast images can be artfully reproduced.

High-contrast copy film. Kodak's high-contrast panchromatic film used for reproducing maps and drawings.

High-contrast developer. A chemical used to enhance the tonal separation for film exposed wrong or for special effects. Some high-contrast developers include FR E-91, Kodak's HC-110, and the ultrahigh-contrast lith developers used with orthochromatic and lith films.

High-energy developer. A specially balanced chemical formula that compensates for underexposure by concentrating on the highlights of a picture. Also called superadditive development.

Highlight areas. The light areas of an image, which reflect the most light. Bright whites in a subject often reflect so much light that the highlight areas in the image appear blank and lack detail. A good photograph is considered to be one that has detail in both the lightest highlight areas and the deepest shadows.

Highlight density. The thickness of the silver build-up in the lightest areas of the image. Sometimes highlights become so dense that detail is lost because of the excessive silver. The density is often used to judge the acceptability of a negative for printing.

High-speed developer. Used to reduce developing time and to build up density and contrast. Unfortunately, the cut in developing time often results in a loss of quality, owing to an increased build-up of grain.

Hot shoe. An electric connection for a flash attachment that does away with the nuisance of a *PC cord.* Connection is made between the flash and the metal surface of the shoe and is transmitted to the camera.

Hyperfocal distance. The range in which objects appear acceptably sharp when a lens is focused at infinity.

Hypersensitizing. A method used to increase an emulsion's *sensitivity* chemically. This may be done either before exposure or after exposure and before development.

Hypo. A common name for fixer, the chemical used to stop development of film and paper. This is actually a misnomer, which resulted from early photographers' assumption that the chemical they were using was sodium hyposulfate. They were close, because the chemical is actually sodium thiosulfate. By the time the mistake was realized, the word hypo had been and still is widely used.

Hypo clearing agent. Speeds washing time of film and paper by facilitating the removal of fixer. Also referred to as hypo eliminator.

Hypo eliminator. See *Hypo clearing agent.*

Image. The visible forms produced by light interacting with a photographic emulsion.

Imagon lens. Trademark for a lens with a special sievelike diaphragm, which produces petaled stars around light sources in a photograph. The lens is made by Rodenstock.

Incident light meter. A gauge that reads the amount of light hitting an object from the direction of the camera. Most hand-held meters can be converted quickly from reflected to incident-type meters by using a *hemispherical diffuser*.

Index of refraction. Used to measure the ability of a piece of glass to bend light. The index of refraction varies with the color of light passing through the piece of glass. Also called refractive index.

Indicator stop-bath. Dilute glacial acetic acid with an added dye that changes color to indicate when the stop-bath is exhausted.

Infrared. Rays with wavelengths longer than those of visible light. Infrared rays make up the part of the electromagnetic spectrum that is sensed as heat and are reflected in varying degrees by almost all objects. The shorter length infrared rays can be photographed with specially formulated black and white or color films, which produce a dramatically different range of tones than those sensed by the human eye. Infrared film is mainly used medically and scientifically to record normally invisible phenomena such as water pollution, diseased plants, and the early growth of some tumors.

Inhibition process. See *Dye transfer process.*

Integrating meter. A type of light meter that reads an average of all the light either reflected or incident on a scene. Most meters, except for spot meters, are integrating and record an average of all the light falling within their angle of coverage. This can be a disadvantage in situations where the lighting either is not ideal or you would like to use a bright spot for a dramatic effect, because the meter will only give an average, integrated reading.

Intensifier. A chemical used to bring up a faint image on underdeveloped film. Intensifier, usually a combination of mercuric iodide with potassium iodide and either sodium sulfite or thiosulfate added, deposits additional particles of metal on the image to make it darker. Intensifiers build on the darkest parts the fastest and also increase contrast. Also called chemical intensifier.

Internal reflection. See *Flare.*

Inter-negative. A color negative made from a slide. Inter-negatives are necessary when enlargements are made with conventional processing methods. There are some processes, such as the Cibachrome process, in which the slide can be printed directly without a negative.

Interval timer. A clock used to time development and fixing of film and prints. One popular type of interval timer measures seconds with a sweep hand and minutes with a second hand. Interval timers also have buzzers to indicate that the time is up.

Inverted telephoto lens. A lens in which the element order is reversed to achieve an opposite effect. One example of an inverted telephoto lens is a fish-eye lens.

Iris diaphragm. Designed after the iris in the human eye, this type of diaphragm consists of thin metal leaves that fold over each other to reduce the size of the aperture.

Kodalith. Trademark for Kodak's lith film and developer.

Lamp. The light source used in either an enlarger or a projector.

Lantern slide. A mounted transparency.

Large format camera. A camera that uses sheets of film to produce 4 × 5, 8 × 10, and sometimes larger negatives.

These cameras are almost always used in a studio because of their size and are almost all *view cameras*. The advantages of film this size are obvious—prints can be made quickly by contact printing, and enlargements are relatively grain-free because of the size of the negatives.

Latent image. See *Developable image.*

Latitude. The room for error built into a film. As a rule, black and white film has a wider exposure latitude than color film.

Leaf shutter. Similar to the *iris diaphragm*, the leaf shutter consists of overlapping thin metal leaves that remain closed until the shutter release is pushed. The leaves then spring open and shut in the amount of time set on the shutter speed dial. A leaf shutter is usually located inside the lens. Also called a blade shutter.

LED. See *Light emitting diode.*

Lens cap. A protective covering used on the back and front of a lens to shield the elements from dust, dirt, scratches, and fingerprints.

Lens coating. The chemical used on *coated lenses.*

Lens elements. Pieces of ground optical glass that combine to make a photographic lens. Early lenses consisted of only two elements, the minimum number necessary to correct distortions. Modern lenses usually combine at least four and sometimes more elements to correct distortions and increase versatility. Also called optical elements.

Lens extender. See *Tele-extender.*

Lens hood. A shield used on the front of a lens to cut down on light flare. The extra rays of the sun on a bright day can pass into the sides of the lens front and create unwanted distortions.

Lens mount. The mechanism used to hold a lens on a camera.

Lens opening. See *f/stop*.

Lens shade. See *Baffle*.

Lever standoff. The distance the re-wind lever stands away from the camera when the film is being advanced. A shorter standoff is less likely to get in the way of your nose (this is not a problem in a twin-lens reflex camera).

Light balancing filters. Used to correct the color cast of light to correspond with the norm represented by the film. For example, light balancing filters can be used to correct early morning or late afternoon light to the color of standard daylight.

Light distribution. The spread of light throughout the film plane. Uneven light distribution of a lens results in dark edges and corners and is particularly noticeable in color film.

Light Emitting Diode (LED). A type of diode that glows when charged with electricity. Different diodes glow with different colors. Light emitting diodes are used in the view-finder of a camera to indicate the meter reading of a built-in light meter. In automatic cameras, LEDs are also used to indicate the proper shutter speed or aperture to use for an exposure.

Light fall-off. Uneven distribution of light over the entire film plane. This can be caused either by a faulty lens or by a flash gun with too narrow an angle. Fall-off is common when an electronic flash is used with a wide-angle lens.

Light meter. A photoelectric exposure gauge that measures light falling on or reflected from an object. Light meters are divided into three basic types: those that are built

into the camera, those that are held in the hand for operation, and those that clip onto the outside of the camera.
Power for a light meter is obtained from a selenium cell, a
cadmium sulfide (CdS) cell, or a variety of diodes powered
by a small battery. Each cell converts light to electric energy and activates a needle on the gauge or a series of LEDs
to indicate the light level. Also called an exposure meter.

Light piping. (1) See *Light streaking.* (2) The method used
to get light inside tiny areas, such as the inside of the
human body. Light is piped into a small cavity through
flexible cords made of glass fibers. The cords are tipped with
tiny fish-eye lenses capable of viewing the entire area.
Several years ago, a Swedish photographer working for *Life*
magazine, Lennart Nilsson, used this method to photograph
the inner ear, a fat-clogged artery, and a living embryo
inside the womb.

Light streaking. Partial fogging of film caused by light
leaking into a film cassette or light in the darkroom while
the film is being loaded into the developing tanks. Actual
streaks of overexposed emulsion appear after the con-
taminated film is developed. The only way to prevent this is
to be extraordinarily careful in the darkroom and in loading
your own film cassettes. Also called light piping.

Light table. A piece of glass with a a light source mounted
underneath. The glass is usually frosted to cut glare and
mounted on a frame similar to a table. Smaller versions of a
light table can be constructed to sit on a table or desk top.
Light tables serve many purposes in special fields of
photography and graphic arts, such as retouching and
opaqueing of negatives and alignment of images.

Line conversion. A high-contrast photograph used to
produce an image resembling a pen-and-ink line drawing.
Duplicate positive and negative high contrast film images
are placed together base to base and contacted onto another
piece of high-contrast lith film. To produce the fine line

image, the sandwiched negative and positive is tilted at an angle during the exposure.

Line film. An image shot on lith film which contains no gray tones. Line negatives are made with a process camera and are used in offset and silk-screen printing.

Lith developer. Specially formulated developer for use with lith films. Lith developer does not allow light gray images to develop. Also called graphic arts developer.

Lith film. High-contrast black and white sheet film used to create images without any gradual tonal separations. Lith film, manufactured under various brand names, such as Kodalith, Cronalith, Formolith, Preprolith, and Gevalith, is not sensitive to blue or green light and records only dark, black or red images. The most common use for lith film is in making halftones and line negatives for offset printing. However, the same lith film and developer is used to create special ultrahigh-contrast negatives for special-effect photography. Also called graphic arts film.

Local reduction. Use of *reducer* on small areas of a negative or print. Reducer can be brushed or dabbed on prints to bring up details lost in shadows while developing for the highlights and can remove unwanted portions of a negative. Drastic local reduction can alter an image and create things you didn't know were there, such as in the famous Steichen portrait of J.P. Morgan, in which the financier seems to be holding a dagger in his hand. In reality, the dagger is a carefully controlled highlight on the arm of his chair.

Localized development. See *Selective development.*

Long-focus lens. See *Telephoto lens.*

Long scale film. One that is capable of reproducing a broad range of gray tones between black and white, such as panchromatic film.

Low-contrast developer. A specially balanced developer used to decrease contrast. When you know that the lighting used will produce too harsh a contrast in the final picture, use of a low-contrast developer such as Ethol TEC or Neofin Blue helps to equalize the contrast of the final print.

Low-voltage-cell unit. A type of electronic flash, which is powered by regular D, C, or AA size batteries.

Lumen seconds. A measurement of the light produced by an electronic flash.

Luminance. The amount of light produced by a light source.

M-synchronization. A shutter synchronization built into the camera and intended for use with a bulb-type flash unit.

Mackie lines. Named after Alexander Mackie, who first described them, Mackie lines are the light bands formed between the highlight and shadow areas of a solarized image.

Macro. When this term is seen alone, it can refer to either the lens used in macrophotography or the picture itself. The strict delineation of where macro ends and micro begins is based on the image size. A macrophotograph must not be more than 10 times life-size. If it is, it is considered a photomicrograph.

Macrophotography. The branch of close-up photography that produces life-size or larger than life-size images. If the images are 10 or more times larger than life, they are called photomicrographs and are usually produced with the aid of a microscope.

Magazine. A cartride that holds a large amount of film. Most magazines are used with a motor drive unit and can hold up to 1500 frames of film.

Magazine-loading device. A piece of equipment that loads film into a bulk film magazine used with a motor drive system.

Magenta. The red primary used in the processes that produce color prints and slides. The other two primaries are cyan (blue) and yellow.

Magnifier. A focusing aid, which can be clipped onto the back of the camera for fine-focusing with a single-lens reflex camera. Focusing magnifiers are commonly used with large view-finder cameras in portrait studios.

Mailers. Envelopes that can be purchased for processing color film. The mailers are sent to the laboratory with the film to indicate that processing was paid in advance. Also called processing mailers.

Manual diaphragm. When used manually, the diaphragm closes as the lens is stopped down, whereas an automatic diaphragm stays open until the shutter is triggered.

Manual override. Feature of automatic cameras that allows for normal operation and setting of both shutter and aperture.

Masking. Blocking part of an image with an opaque object or film. Masking may be used in multiple exposures to selectively add to a transparency or in printing to block out undesirable parts of a negative. When used with an enlarger or copy camera, a transparent red film called rubylith is usually used.

Matte surface. A printing paper with a dull or low-luster finish. Matte surface papers lack the depth of high gloss but have none of the hard brilliance or glare that also accompanies shininess.

Metallic silver. During development, the silver compounds in the film's emulsion are broken up, and the resulting particles of silver—the metallic silver—form the image on the film.

Mezzotint. See *Screen tint.*

Micro. A shortened term for *Photomicrography.*

Microdol-X. Trademark for a fine-grain developer manufactured by Kodak for use with black and white film.

Microgrid. A small round spot used for focusing inside the viewing screen of some single-lens reflex cameras. The microgrid, or microprism grid as it is properly called, contains many tiny triangles, which appear to shimmer when the subject is out of focus. As the subject is brought into focus, these triangles line up until the image is clearly focused.

Microprism. A focusing system used in some cameras, commonly called a *microgrid.*

Microprism grid. See *Microgrid.*

Middle-tone. (1) An average gray tone in regular black and white photography. (2) The intermediate tones produced by *posterization.*

Mini-pod. A small tripod used on a tabletop or flat surface for close-up photography or other close work for which the standard tripod would be too cumbersome.

Mirror adapter. A handy accessory, which can be attached to some long lenses to allow the photographer to see around corners. The mirror adapter contains a 45-degree reflex mirror.

Mirror damping. Special noise-absorbing material used inside a single-lens reflex camera to cut down on the loud clack the mirror makes as it falls down after snapping up out of the way during the exposure.

Mirror telephoto. An ultra-long telephoto lens that has been shortened by using mirrors in its optical design. The result is a very fat lens that can be hand-held. However, the use of mirrors cuts down even further on the depth of field.

mm. Stands for millimeter. The millimeter is the commonly used unit of measurement for film size and focal length.

Modeling. An illusion of depth created by controlling the position and angle of the light source in studio lighting.

Monobath. A combination of developer and fixer. This method is used to drastically cut development time.

Monocular. One-half of a pair of binoculars.

Motor drive. A battery-operated mechanical film advance used to take pictures rapidly or at pre-set times, such as in time-lapse photography. A motor drive system holds enough film for up to 1500 exposures and frees the photographer from constantly advancing the film manually.

Motorized film advance. See *Power winder.*

Mounting flange. A circular piece of metal mounted on the camera body. This flange, which can be threaded or have a bayonet or breechlock, connects the lens securely to the camera and often contains the coupling for a built-in meter.

Mounting press. A heat-controlled press used for dry-mounting photographs.

Multicoated lens. See *Coated lens.*

Multicontrast paper. See *Variable contrast paper.*

Multiflex bellows. See *Bellows.*

Multiple image. This may be a double exposure or any other image created by using several images together.

Multi-vibrator. A unit used to raise the voltage of regular DC current to the level required by an electronic flash unit.

Negative carrier. The part of an enlarger that holds the negative in place during projection. The negative carrier is a removable flat metal frame, which sits between the lens and the condenser.

Negative distortion. See *Pincushion distortion.*

Neutral density filter. Two polarizing screens used together on a lens to reduce exposure when the light is very bright and a high-speed film must be used. Neutral density filters are available in several densities for transmitting from 90 to 1/100 percent of the light.

Neutral gray card. A gray piece of cardboard, also called an 18-percent reflectance card, used to determine an exposure with a light meter.

Neutralization. The action of an acid-based formula on a basic solution. Acetic acid is employed as a stop-bath to neutralize the basic developer used for prints and negatives. This neutralization abruptly halts development of the image.

Nickel cadmium battery. A rechargeable battery used to store energy in an electronic flash.

Normal lens. The lens that usually comes on a camera. The focal length of a normal lens is roughly equal to the diagonal measure of the film used in the camera. For 35mm film, this would be about 50 mm. A normal lens approximates the human field of vision. Also called the prime lens or standard lens.

Opacity. The thickness or density of the silver layer,

which determines the amount of light that can get through a negative.

Opaque. A black or red paint used to cover pinholes in high-contrast negatives. Light will not pass through areas of a negative that have been painted with opaque.

Optical elements. See *Lens elements.*

Optics. (1) The branch of physics that deals with the transmission of light through lenses. (2) The attributes of a lens and its freedom from aberrations. Lenses with "good optics" are always more expensive.

Orthochromatic emulsion. A photosensitive emulsion used in paper and films that is sensitive to all colors except red. Its widest use is in the graphic arts trade for making halftones and line negatives on lith film.

Pan film. Shortened term for *Panchromatic film.*

Panchromatic film. Black and white film that is sensitive to all colors of light. Also called pan film.

Panning. Slowly turning (1) a motion picture camera to take in an entire scene or (2) a still camera to create a sense of motion in a photograph.

Panoramic cameras. Special cameras that can cover a wide viewing area in one shot. The lens swings from side to side during the exposure. Because of the wide angle of the photograph, panoramic photographs show cylindrical perspective if there are any definite verticals in the picture.

Paper. A commonly used term for *Enlarging paper.*

Paper grades. The numbers used on photographic paper to indicate how much contrast the emulsion can produce. The lower the number, the lower the contrast of the paper, and the more gray tones produced.

Paper negative. A reversed print made on photographic paper by direct contact printing with a positive print. This paper negative can be contacted to another piece of photographic paper to create a greatly softened image.

Paper safe. A light-proof box used to store photographic paper in a darkroom. Paper may be removed from the box under the protective illumination of a safelight.

Parallax. The slight difference between the picture seen through a view-finder on a range-finder camera and the actual image produced on the film. This difference, usually called parallax error, is corrected on expensive range-finder cameras but not on the inexpensive, instamatic type. Parallax error accounts for the headless phenomenon common to family snapshots.

Parallax compensator. Used with a lens-coupled range-finder camera to correct parallax error in the view finder.

Parallax error. Those mistakes you always seem to make with a range-finder camera. Whenever you try to get in Uncle Albert's feet, you somehow always chop off his head. Better luck next time. See *Parallax*.

PC connection. A small electrical socket built into most cameras. The PC connection is specially designed to connect an electronic flash with the shutter mechanism.

PC cord. A nuisance that always seems to be in front of the camera or else not tightly connected. This is the cord which connects the flash with the camera through the PC connection. Also called a sync cord.

Penlights. See *AA cells*.

Pentaprism. A five-sided lens that sits at the top of a

single-lens reflex camera and directs the image reflected on a mirror from the camera's lens through the view finder for focusing.

Perceptol. Trademark for Ilford's fine-grain developer.

Perspective. The relation in size and location of objects, which imparts a sense of depth and distance in a picture.

Petzval sum. See under *Astigmatism.*

Photo eye. See *Slave unit.*

Photoelectric meter. A light meter that measures light through a cell powered by a battery.

Photoflash lamp. See *Flash bulb.*

Photoflood. A brilliant light used in a photographic studio. Photofloods are usually mounted in reflectors to concentrate the light.

Photogram. A direct photographic impression made by placing an object on top of printing paper and exposing it to light. The object blocks out the light where it is solid and leaves an outline, or shadow picture.

Photographic level. Similar to the device used by builders, a photographic level helps a photographer to determine whether the film plane is on the same vertical plane as the subject. This type of level is used mostly in reproducing works of art hung in a museum.

Photographic paper. See *Enlarging paper.*

Photometer. Any instrument used in *photometry.* One example of a photometer is a densitometer.

Photometry. The physical science which deals with the

measure of the intensity of light. The most commonly used photometric measure in photography is the foot-candle.

Photomicrography. Close-up photography in which the subject is reproduced more than ten times life-size. Commonly referred to as "micro" work.

Photomontage. A collection of pictures, clippings from magazines, and other materials, combined to make an abstract image or to alter the reality in a picture. This montage is then photographed and printed in the ordinary way. The result is often a photograph that looks like an absurd or impossible reality. Photomontage was a popular form of photography with surrealist artists such as Man Ray, Max Ernst, and John Heartfield.

Photon. A particle of radiant energy that when traveling at the speed of light is visible to the human eye. Photons make up rays of light when traveling at the proper speed and wavelength.

Photosensitive. Sensitive to light. A material is said to be photosensitive if it reacts to light in such a way that it actually changes. In photography, photosensitive materials are those that alter their structure to allow a chemical reaction with the silver compounds in an emulsion. This produces a negative.

Physical development. A process in which silver is deposited on the latent image from a solution of silver salts and developing agents. This deposit of silver creates the image.

Pigment process. Any photographic process that uses a pigment to help produce the image, such as gum, oil, bromoil, or carbon printing.

Pin registration. A method of *film registration* in which the pieces of film and images are aligned by using plastic or meta! pins to hold the film in place on the baseboard of the enlarger.

Pincushion distortion. A lens aberration in which vertical and horizontal straight lines appear to bow inward. Also called negative distortion.

Pinhole. A small hole in the opaque parts of a negative. Pinholes can be a result of dust or dirt on the film or on the exposure equipment such as the contact printer. Pinholes are not a problem with regular roll film because this film is encased in a dust-proof container; however, when duplicate or high-contrast negatives are made, dust can mar the film's emulsion. Pinholes are also common in high-contrast negatives but can be easily repaired with liquid opaque.

Pinhole camera. An early sophistication of the camera obscura. Instead of a room, a box of manageable size was used. Film was placed in the rear of the box and exposed through the pinhole, creating a blurred image.

Pistol-grip. A camera support that features a contoured grip similar to that found on a pistol. This support rests on the shoulder and allows greater control of the camera. It also helps to support long telephoto lenses.

Plane of focus. See *Focal plane.*

Plugged film. A combination of overexposure and over-development, which causes the image to "plug up," or build up a heavy silver deposit in the highlight and shadow areas. Plugging of film is similar to *blocking up.*

Plus-X. Trademark for a black and white film with an ASA of 125. Plus-X is manufactured by Kodak.

Polarization. The screening of light waves so that they undulate in one direction only. Polarization, which is done with a special polarizing filter, can help to control reflections, improve the brightness of the sky for color photography, and control contrast. Polarizing filters or screens can also be used in pairs to form a *neutral density filter* for controlling the amount of light used for an exposure.

Polarizing filter. A screen made up of submicroscopic crystals lined up in parallel lines. A polarizing filter is used to screen out light angled in directions different than the parallel grid of the screen. Although this type of filter appears transparent, the aperture must be opened an additional 1⅓ stops to allow for light blockage.

Polaroid Land film. A special film used to produce both a negative and a positive print at the same time. A recent Polaroid film does the entire operation on one paper in broad daylight.

Polycontrast filters. Magenta and yellow filters of varying densities used with variable contrast paper. Polycontrast is Kodak's trademark for variable contrast.

Polycontrast paper. Trademark for a variable contrast printing paper manufactured by Kodak.

Portrait lens. A special lens used to take formal pictures of people. Some portrait lenses are slightly longer in focal length to allow the photographer to get a good head and shoulders shot without breathing down the subject's throat. Others are soft-focus lenses to create a softer, more ethereal effect.

Positive. An image in which either the gray tones or colors correspond with what the eye expects to see. In other words, the whites are white and the blacks black, as opposed to a negative image.

Positive distortion. See *Barrel distortion.*

Posterization. A high-contrast technique in which the

tones are rendered in sharply defined gradations. Posterizations may have two, three, four or more distinct tones.

Potassium alum. A hardening agent added to fixer to prevent the film emulsion from swelling or softening during washing.

Potassium ferricyanide. A chemical used to reduce the metallic silver in a photographic image. This is often called reducer.

Potentiometer. The part of a camera that is controlled by the ASA setting and that keys the light meter response to the film speed. In automatic cameras, the potentiometer also keys either the shutter speed or aperture, depending on the camera's priority.

Power pack. A large, 510-volt dry cell battery that operates an electronic flash. This battery is carried in a case slung over the shoulder, with a flash unit connected to the power pack by a tightly coiled cord.

Power winder. An auxiliary device now available for many cameras that frees the photographer from manually advancing the film. Winders are usually run on batteries and attach to the bottom of a single-lens reflex camera. Also called a winder, auto-winder, or motorized film advance.

Pre-exposure. A technique to fill in shadow detail on Polaroid black and white prints. A first exposure, or pre-exposure, is taken from a *gray card.* This extends the inherently short tonal range of the film by filling in detail on highlights without overexposing the film and by extending the range into the dark areas for shadow detail.

Preservative. A chemical added to developer to increase the life of the solution by retarding oxidation.

Preset diaphragm. A diaphragm mechanism that allows

you to select an aperture, focus at the full aperture for maximum brightness, then turn a pre-set ring when you are ready to shoot. The pre-set ring stops down the lens until you open it manually.

Press camera. A portable version of the view camera, once widely used by newspaper photographers but now largely supplanted by the more portable single-lens reflex camera. Some diehards still insist on the old press camera for certain news and sports events. Also called a Speed Graphic.

Pre-view lever. A lever used to manually stop down a lens to check on depth of field in automatic lenses.

Prime lens. See *Normal lens.*

Print file sheets. Clear, plastic sleeves used to file prints for reference or in a portfolio. The plastic protects the photograph and allows a clear view.

Print timer. Used to time development and agitation of photographic prints.

Printing box. Similar to a contact printing frame, a printing box has a built-in light source as well as a frame and tight-fitting top. A printing box is used with large-format film, such as 4 × 5 and larger, to make contact prints.

Printing gamma. A relationship between the paper's sensitivity and the proper development time for an image.

Printing paper. See *Enlarging paper.*

Process camera. A large view-camera, which can enlarge or reduce an image for reproduction on lith film.

Process emulsion. A high-contrast emulsion used for specialty photography and in the graphic arts industry. Lith film is one example of a process emulsion.

Processing mailers. See *Mailers.*

Processor. Shortened term for *Stabilization processor.*

Professional film. Color print or slide film that is released at the aim point, or point of maximum color quality, for critical, professional color photography. Professional color film should be refrigerated until it is used and processed immediately to retain the advantage of the aim point.

Projection printer. See *Enlarger.*

Projector. A machine with a light source, condenser, and magnifying lens, used to project images of transparencies on a flat surface. Most projectors are designed for standard 2 × 2-inch slides and come with a variety of slide magazines. Other options in projectors include automatic focus control, zoom lenses, and remote control devices.

Proof sheet. See *Contact sheet.*

Pushing film. Deliberately underexposing the film and then compensating by special development. The underexposure is regulated by the ASA setting, which also serves as a guide for development. Pushing film results in a loss of contrast in black and white and an altered color balance in color film because of the lengthened development. Both film types also suffer an increase in grain.

Quartz adapter. Used to convert a standard photoflood to a quartz halogen lamp. The adapter screws into the photo flood socket and accepts any two-prong quartz halogen bulb.

Quartz-iodine lamp. A continuous-light source for studio photography. Each lamp has a sealed quartz glass tube with a tungsten filament and iodine inside. Electric current vaporizes the tungsten, which glows at a steady brilliance and temperature for up to 30 hours. Quartz-iodine lamps are also convenient because they can produce as much light as four photofloods when used with reflectors.

Rack and pinion. The same technology that gives you fast-cornering sports cars also supports an enlarger. The rack and pinion control mechanism in an enlarger consists of a geared track operated by a knob or wheel and provides the same accurancy and reliability as rack and pinion steering in a car.

Radiant light. Direct illumination from a light source such as a photoflood, flash gun, or the sun.

Range-finder. See *Coupled range-finder.*

Range-finder focusing system. See *Coupled range-finder.*

Rapid developer. A chemical used to develop negatives faster than normal. The drawbacks of rapid developers are increased grain and higher contrast.

Rapid-fixer. Specially formulated fixer that acts in less time than the conventional product.

Rapid Rectilinear lens. See *Aplanat lens.*

Rayograph. A *photogram* made by placing objects, both opaque and translucent, on photographic paper. This type of photogram was dubbed a rayograph by none other than Man Ray, a surrealist artist, even though another artist, Christian Schad, had already dubbed it the schadograph.

Ready light. A small red or amber square mounted on the back or side of an electronic flash, which lights up when the capacitor is fully charged. The ready light is used to indicate that the unit is ready for another flash.

Recording film. Very high speed film used for low light level situations.

Rectilinear perspective. Perspective in which straight lines are reproduced as straight lines, whether vertical or horizontal or parallel. Angles also retain their true shape in rectilinear perspective.

Recycling time. The time required for an electronic flash unit to collect enough energy from the battery for a full discharge of light. An indicator lights up when the unit has recycled, usually within 7 to 20 seconds. Longer recycling times indicate that the battery is wearing down and must either be recharged or replaced.

Red-eye. The result of staring directly at a flash mounted on the camera, red eye is a common occurrence in color photography. It is the reflection of the blood vessels in the retina and should be discouraged by having the subject look slightly away from the flash gun.

Reducer. A chemical, usually potassium ferricyanide, used to reduce the silver build-up on a negative or print. Reducer may be used on the whole image or selectively brushed on for special effects.

Reducing. Using a chemical reducer to remove part of the silver on a developed black and white negative or print.

Reference strip. A standardized collection of color prints indicating imbalances in color. A reference strip is invaluable to the novice color printer for determining which filters should be used to correct the color tone.

Reflectance. The amount of light reflected from a subject and recorded on film. Reflectance determines the density of the highlight and shadow areas on a negative.

Reflected-light meter. A light meter that reads the amount of light reflected off a subject.

Reflex camera. A camera that reflects the image with a

mirror for focusing. In all reflex cameras, the mirror first changes the direction of the light from horizontal to vertical. The light is then directed upward to either a viewing screen or a pentaprism. In the latter case, as in single-lens reflex cameras, the pentaprism then directs the light back to the horizontal for easy focusing by the photographer.

Reforming. After recharging a depleted electronic flash, the capacitor must be reformed, or re-educated, to put out the maximum amount of energy for each flash. This is accomplished in the same way as *forming:* several flashes in succession are discharged, and the unit is left to recharge. This process is repeated two or three times until the unit seems to be working properly. If the capacitor is not properly reformed, it may not be able to accept a full charge of energy.

Refraction. As light passes at an angle from a medium of one density, (such as air) through a medium of a different density (such as water or glass), it is bent, or refracted, at an angle varying with the wavelength of the light and the density of the medium. The difference in the refraction of light of varying colors is called *dispersion.*

Refractive index. See *Index of refraction.*

Relative aperture. See *f/stop.*

Remote sensor. A device used with a *bounce flash* to control exposure. The sensor records only what the camera sees, eliminating extraneous light.

Replenishment. Restoration of developer or fixer for longer use. Special chemicals can be added to either solution after use to prolong its effectiveness and to cut costs.

Reprolith. Trademark for GAF's lith film and developer.

Resolution. The ability of a lens to produce a clear image with good edge sharpness. The resolving power of a lens varies with the test object used, the light used to illuminate the test object, the aperture, and the person conducting the test. The resolution of a film emulsion is tested in much the same way.

Resolving power. The measure of *resolution* of a lens.

Restrainer. Chemical added to developer to keep the image from forming too fast. If the image were to form too fast, highlight and shadow detail would be lost due to a heavy silver deposit.

Reticulation. Crinkling of the film emulsion, which occurs when a negative is abruptly moved from a very warm to a very cold solution. The even, permanent pattern formed in the emulsion can be used artistically but is usually considered a defect.

Reversal. A slide made with *color-reversal film*.

Reverse adapter. A ring used to mount a lens on a camera backward. By mounting the lens backward, you create a simple macro lens, which will slightly enlarge a subject and focus closer than normal.

Ring light. See *Flash ring*.

Roll film. Film that is packed in specified lengths and backed with opaque paper for protection against light.

Rotary dryer. A machine used to dry prints after washing. The prints are carried around a heated metal drum until they are dry.

Rotating prism. A triangular lens used to focus the image in a coupled range-finder system.

Rubylith. Trademark for a red masking film manufactured by Ulano Co. Rubylith is used to mask out unwanted areas on negatives or prints.

Sabattier effect. Commonly misnamed solarization, the Sabattier effect is a partial reversal of an image from positive to negative by briefly flashing a light on a print while it is in the developer. A true solarization would completely reverse the image. One result of the Sabattier effect is a light outline around the solarized object. These are *Mackie lines.*

Safelight. A colored light that does not affect photographic paper. Safelights are used in the darkroom to observe development progress. The most popular colors are amber, green, and red.

Sandwiching. Layering transparencies, either black and white or color, for special effects. The same result can be achieved in the camera by double-exposure.

Scale. Size relationship of objects in a photograph.

Scale of a film. Terminology used to refer to the film's ability to reproduce a range of gray tones. The more gray tones produced by a film, the longer the scale is said to be.

Scatter. The internal reflection of a small portion of light. In a lens, this effect is called flare. It is also present to some degree in film, where it is called halation. Light scatters through the image, reducing contrast and creating ghost images.

Schadograph. A photogram of various objects placed on printing paper and exposed, creating a shadow image of the montage. This technique was named by Christian Schad, a surrealist artist.

Screen-produced star. A pointed rendition of a small bright light source in a photograph. A screen-produced star is obtained by using a screen in front of the lens, as one would place a filter. A single screen produces a four-pointed star, and a double screen placed at an angle to the first produces eight-pointed stars.

Screen tint. High contrast or continous-tone patterns printed on film, which can be used to modify or change tones in a print. Screen tints are either dotted or patterned to produce a variety of textures in the print. Also called mezzotint.

Secondary spectrum. Residual wavelengths of light not corrected in an achromatic lens. These other wavelengths usually focus very close to the corrected wavelengths and are of little or no consequence in most cases. If a lens has further reduced the secondary spectrum by bringing three colors to a common focus, it is referred to as an apochromat.

Sectional enlargement. A print made from a small piece of a negative. This is often done to eliminate unwanted parts of a picture. However, if the section of the negative enlarged is very small and the print very large, the enlargement will probably appear very grainy.

Selective development. Certain parts of a print may seem to need more development than others, especially if they are finely detailed. They can be selectively developed by being rubbed gently with a finger while the print is in the developer. The heat generated by your body and the friction of rubbing speed development in a particular area. This process is also called localized development.

Selective focus. One part of a picture which is in focus for a special effect. This can be accomplished by using a large aperture or a long lens.

Selective solarization. Controlled re-exposure of a photographic image to white light. All the areas of the print that you don't want solarized are covered during this re-exposure.

Selenium cell. A type of photoelectric light sensor used in some light meters.

Selenium toner. A dye used to enrich the blacks and brighten the whites in a black and white print. Selenium toner gives a "colder" effect to the paper.

Self-timer. A gizmo found on many cameras that delays the shutter for several seconds while you run around and get into the picture.

Semiautomatic diaphragm. A mechanism on some lenses that allows you to reopen the aperture with a special lever after the diaphragm has been shut down. This type of diaphragm makes it possible to focus freely with a bright screen. When you trigger the shutter, the diaphragm automatically closes to the pre-set aperture until you open it manually.

Semispot. A type of light meter that reads the light in a small area of a scene. A semispot meter does not have as narrow a spot for reading as a regular spot meter.

Sensing cell. The photoelectric part of a light meter, which measures the amount of light either incident on or reflected from an object.

Sensitivity. Refers to an emulsion's ability to react to light. Films and papers that need less light to produce an image are considered more sensitive.

Sensitometer. A machine used to precisely control the exposure of the same image when it is photographed several times.

Sensitometry. The measure of light sensitivity. Photographic sensitometry varies with several factors, including: knowledge of the spectral characteristics of the source of radiation; controlled development; measurement of density; and proper interpretation of results.

Separations. (1) Negatives or positives exposed at different levels to create the intermediate tones of posterization. (2) The negatives used in four-color printing processes. These negatives are shot through filters that separate the colors.

Shadow area. The dark area of an image, which reflects the least amount of light. Often, in photographs with bright areas, detail in the shadow area is lost due to relative underexposure. A good photograph is generally considered to be one with both shadow and highlight detail.

Sharpness. The clarity or *acutance* of an image produced by a lens.

Sheet film. Used in view cameras, sheet film sizes include 4 × 5 inches and 8 × 10 inches. They generally come in boxes of 10 or 25, and each sheet is separated by black paper. Also called cut film.

Shirley. Standardized test negative used for color balancing. Since facial tones are a good reference point for color printing, Shirleys are pictures of models and were presumably named after the first model.

Shoe-mount. See *Hot shoe.*

Short-focus lens. See *Wide-angle lens.*

Short lighting. A placement of the main light for portrait photography. In short lighting the main light is positioned so that it illuminates the side of the face away from the camera. This type of lighting brings out facial contours and can be used to de-emphasize the width of plump faces.

Short scale film. A film that reproduces few or no gray tones between solid black and white. An example of a short scale film is the lith film used for high-contrast negatives.

Shoulder-pod. A camera prop that uses the shoulder as one point of support.

Shutter. The mechanism in a camera which controls the amount of time that light can reach the film. The two main types in common use are the leaf and focal plane shutters.

Shutter priority. Describes an automatic exposure control camera in which the shutter speed is manually controlled.

Shutter release. The button or knob that activates the shutter.

Silica gel. Packaged in small paper envelopes, this chemical is used to absorb excess moisture in camera equipment. Most cameras come with one or two of these envelopes tucked into their cases to retard moisture in shipping. Hold onto these for your own storage or when you are traveling.

Silicon blue cell. A type of light-sensitive cell used in a light meter. Silicon cells are similar to CdS cells, except that they have eliminated the memory defect characteristic of the CdS. The overall response of a silicon cell is also much faster; however, this type of cell is particularly sensitive to infrared light and must be heavily filtered to prevent unbalanced readings.

Silver bromide. The most commonly used photosensitive chemical for a film emulsion.

Silver halide. Chemical terminology for any of the photosensitive silver compounds.

Silver iodide. This chemical compound formed the image in the early daguerreotypes and calotypes. Although a trace of it is still added to some film emulsions, it is generally considered to be too slow acting for modern photography.

Silver nitrate. A photosensitive silver compound used in early photographic experiments.

Single-lens reflex camera (SLR). One of the most popular types of camera on the market today, the single-lens reflex has enabled a large number of amateur photographers to produce work that is sometimes on a par with that of professional photographers. The single-lens reflex allows the photographer to view and focus his subject directly through the lens, without any annoying parallax error.

The SLR system works as follows: a light-reflecting mirror directs the image upward through a pentaprism, which bounces the image around until it is right-side up and facing out toward the viewer's eye. Because the mirror used to reflect the image through the pentaprism obstructs the path of light to the film, it must swing upward to be out of the way for an exposure. So the mirror falls back into position with a characteristic audible click, making the single-lens reflex one of the noisier cameras. However, most of this noise is dampened and is definitely offset by the many advantages the camera offers. One of these advantages is the ability to view directly through a lens of any focal length for telephoto or wide-angle work. A single-lens reflex camera also makes micro and macro photography much easier because the tiny objects, with their shallow depth of field, can be directly focused.

Single weight. See *SW*.

Skylight filter. A pale pink filter that does not affect the light transmission of a lens but shields the front element from dust, dirt, water, and fingerprints during shooting. A skylight filter also slightly warms the tones in color photography.

Slave unit. A small auxiliary flash unit used in a studio set-up. Also called a photo eye.

Slide. (1) A method of adjusting the front and back of a view camera to correct perspective in a two-dimensional picture. (2) A *transparency*.

Slide copier. A set-up that allows you to duplicate your own slides. The slide copier consists of a special bellows, a copier rod equipped with a diffuser glass, and an acceptable light source. Also called a slide duplicator.

Slide duplicator. See *Slide copier.*

Slide masks. Shaped cut-outs used to cover parts of a slide for special effects. Masks can be any shape but are generally round, oval, or geometric.

Slide mount. A cardboard, plastic, or glass holder for a film positive. The mount holds the film flat for good projection.

SLR. Stands for *Single-Lens Reflex.*

Small format camera. Any camera that can use rolls of film, such as 35 mm, Instamatic, or 2¼ cameras. Small format cameras produce negatives that must be enlarged for a final print, as opposed to large format cameras, which produce 4 × 5, 8 × 10, or larger sheet negatives for contact printing.

Snap Cap. Trademark for a film cartridge used with a bulk film loader.

Soft focus lens. A lens that purposely makes the outlines in a picture appear slightly fuzzy. This type of lens is usually used for portrait work to soften the features.

Soft paper. Photographic paper with low contrast.

Solarization. Reversal of an image from negative to positive by briefly flashing it with light. Complete solarization is used with some types of color slide film to reverse the image. In common darkroom parlance, however, a print is considered solarized when it has been flashed with light while in the developer. This partial solarization, which is not true solarization, is properly known as the *Sabattier effect.*

Sound-sync. An added feature of a slide projector that allows a tape recorder to be directly connected to the projector for synchronized sound and sight slide shows.

Soup. Slang term for film developer.

Spectrum. The range of wavelengths of light including all the colors. The visible light spectrum is part of a broader set of energy called the electromagnetic spectrum.

Speed Graphic. See *Press camera.*

Speed index. See *ASA.*

Speedlight. See *Electronic flash.*

Spherical aberration. The failure of light rays to converge at the same point as a result of curvature of the margins of a lens. Spherical aberrations are corrected to a certain degree by combining positive and negative lenses of the proper powers but are never completely eliminated. Since this aberration varies with aperture, it may be reduced by using smaller f/stops.

Spherical diffuser. A lazy man's term for a *hemispherical diffuser.*

Spherical perspective. A distorted perspective common to fish-eye lenses and some animals. In spherical perspective, all vertical lines except for those in the center appear to curve inward, forming a circular image.

Split-field lens. One that can focus two different fields in one frame.

Split image. A focusing system in which the picture is focused by lining up two parts of the image in the view finder.

Spot meter. A light meter that reads an area as narrow as one degree. Because of the small area covered by this type of meter, an object can be pinpointed fairly accurately for a meter reading.

Spotlight. A photoflood mounted slightly out from a metal reflector so that the rays of light converge in a narrow spot.

Spotting. Applying spotting dye to the unsightly white marks left on a photographic print by dust and dirt in the enlarger.

Spotting dye. Black paint used to remove light blemishes from a black and white photograph. Spotting dyes come in a variety of black tones to match just about any type of paper.

Spring cassette. A type of cartridge used with a bulk film loader.

Stabilization paper. A printing paper manufactured for use with a processing machine. Stabilization papers, such as Kodak's Ektamatic series, are developed and fixed inside a processor with activator and stabilizer solutions. This processor can drastically cut development time but does not allow any special control over print development. Also, since the stabilizer is not a permanent fixer, the prints must be manually fixed if they are to be kept for any length of time.

Stabilization processor. A paper processor that automatically develops and stabilizes photographic prints. Special stabilization paper is fed into the machine after exposure. Rollers carry the paper first through an activator bath and then a stabilizer bath. The developed print is then returned to you at the front of the machine. These processors are used for high-volume work, such as in the photo lab of a newspaper, where development time is critical. Another form of this type of processor is used in instant portrait machines that are often seen at amusement parks. Also called, simply, a processor.

Standard lens. See *Normal lens.*

Static eliminator. A type of brush used to control dust on negatives and on camera and enlarger lenses. Static eliminators operate by radioactively discharging the static electricity that holds the dust and dirt on the film or lens surface.

Step-up adapter rings. These gadgets allow use of larger filters on smaller camera mounts. The back of the adapter ring screws into the front of the camera lens, and the front threads accept a larger size filter. This is particularly handy if you have an odd size camera.

Still development. Used with solarized prints, still development is simply processing the paper without agitating the tray or tank after the re-exposure. This method is definitely not recommended for most prints.

Stop. (1) To halt or freeze action by using an electronic flash or a high shutter speed. (2) A shortened term for *f/stop.*

Stop-bath. A weak solution of glacial acetic acid that abruptly halts development. As soon as development is finished, the print is immersed in the acid stop to prevent overdevelopment. Glacial acetic acid is used to counteract the basic properties of developer, but plain water also stops development, although it does so more slowly.

Stop-fix. A chemical used in developing color film and prints, which combines the stop-bath and fixer actions.

Stopping down. Changing the aperture setting of a lens to a smaller opening.

Streak the film. To mar the film surface with chemicals or light. Chemical streaks are the result of improper agitation and/or washing of the film. Light streaks in the developed emulsion are usually caused by light hitting the film while it is still in the cassette or while it is being loaded on the developing reel.

Streaking. Usually caused by a light leak, streaking can also be caused by developer. Chemicals or light can sometimes mar the image with swaths of light-colored emulsion. These swaths, or streaks, can be caused by uneven agitation of film or paper while developing and by uneven fixing of film or paper.

Strobe. See *Electronic flash.*

Subtractive filters. Colored pieces of glass, gelatine, or acetate used to block certain colors of light. Subtractive filters are used in color printing to balance the enlarger light and in the graphic arts industry to create four-color half-tone separations of color photography.

Subtractive process. The method that is the basis for modern color film and processing. In the subtractive process, colors are taken away from white light to get different colors. The standard primaries used in the subtractive process are cyan, magenta, and yellow. When combined in the proper proportions, these primaries absorb all the colors of light to produce black.

Sun shade. See *Baffle.*

Superadditive development. See *High-energy developer.*

Supplementary lens. A simple lens that can be added to the camera's lens to increase or decrease focal length.

SW. Stands for Single Weight. This type of printing paper is of average thickness. Since it is not very heavy, single weight paper tends to curl as it dries.

Sweep-second timer. A clock with two or more hands on its face, one of which measures seconds. *Interval timers* are a type of sweep-second timer.

Swing. A method used to correct perspective with a view camera. Swing is an adjustment of either the front or the back of the camera so that the film plane is on the same angle as the subject.

Sync cord. See *PC cord.*

Sync-shade. An electronic flash used outdoors to fill in light on a subject in deep shade.

Synchro-Sun. An electronic flash used at the same time as sunlight for an exposure.

T. Stands for time. This marking appears on many shutter speed dials and simply indicates the setting used to hold the shutter open for an undetermined time until it is manually closed by releasing the shutter release.

Tacking iron. Used in conjunction with a dry-mounting press, a tacking iron is a metal wand with an internal heating unit. When hot, the iron is applied to the corners of a sheet of waxy dry-mounting paper placed against the back of a photo. This ensures that the paper is flat and in contact with the entire back of the photo for even, flat mounting.

Take a reading. To determine the proper exposure from the indicator on a light meter. Light meter readings are taken while pointing the meter at the subject to measure the reflected or incident light.

Take-up spool. The reel inside a camera that winds up and stores the exposed film until it is removed from the camera for processing.

Tandem flash unit. One that is powered by external power sources in conjunction with an internal fully-charged capacitor.

Tape registration. A simple method of film registration, in which tape is used to hold the sheets of film in place for exposure.

Tele-converter. See *Tele-extender.*

Tele-extender. A small, simple lens that can be screwed onto the front of a regular camera lens to extend the focal length. The tele-extender is used to double or triple (each extender is labeled 2× or 3×, depending on magnification power) the focal length so that a photographer can cheaply and easily have a variety of magnifications from one lens. However, these extenders cut out a great deal of light and increase lens distortions. Also called an auto converter, lens extender, tele-converter, or extender.

Telephoto lens. A lens with a long focal length, which makes objects appear to be closer to the camera than they really are. Most people consider the 135 mm lens to be the beginning of the telephoto lens category in 35 mm photography. The length of the lenses increases rapidly to 200 mm, 400 mm, and upward. A lens longer than 200 mm is almost impossible to use without a tripod, because any slight movement during the shooting of a picture will blur the distant subject. In seeming to bring the object closer to the camera, the telephoto lens compresses distance into a small area, creating the illusion of a very shallow depth of field. This compression of space also distorts the perspective and relative sizes of other objects in the picture. Also called a long-focus lens.

Test strips. Pieces of photographic paper exposed for increments of one, two, three, or more seconds to determine the proper exposure. An opaque piece of cardboard is gradually shifted until the entire strip is exposed. The strip is then developed and fixed just like the final print. Close inspection usually indicates which amount of time should be used for the exposure.

Test wedges. Similar to test strips, test wedges are made on an entire sheet of photographic paper. In this way, you can determine exposure or color balance of an entire photograph rather than a thin portion of it.

Thin negative. One with little metallic silver deposited on the image. This type of negative makes prints with very low contrast and is often impossible to print successfully.

Threaded mount. A type of lens mount in which the lens is screwed onto the camera.

3 × extender. A tele-extender that can triple the magnification power of a lens, creating a longer focal length. For instance, a 3× extender used on a 50 mm lens gives the result of a 150 mm lens.

Thyristor. A semiconductor device used in an automatic electronic flash to control the amount of light emitted in a flash. The thyristor limits the light according to the reading from the electronic eye. This type of unit conserves the charge of the flash.

Tilt. An adjustment of either the front or back of a view camera to correct perspective in a two-dimensional picture. The camera is tilted or swung until the film plane is at the same angle as the subject and the perspective is rendered naturally.

Time exposure. A photograph made by holding the shutter open manually for an undetermined amount of time. Time exposures made at night often render a scene with a rather eerie feeling. Any movement made during the time exposure is recorded as a blur or line, such as car headlights or sparklers on the Fourth of July.

Time-lapse photography. A process in which a timer is set so that the camera is automatically triggered periodically during an interval to obtain pictures of a subject over a longer period of time. Time-lapse photography is used scientifically to record motion too slow to be detected by the human eye, such as plant growth.

Time-O-Lite. Trademark for a popular interval timer.

Timer. A device used to regulate a photographic enlarger. The timer automatically shuts off the enlarger light when the paper has been exposed for the set time. The timer is also used to accurately keep track of the length of film and print development. One other type of timer used in photography is the self-timer, which delays triggering of the camera shutter for several seconds.

Tonal range. The number of gray tones between black and white that are visible in a print; the more gray tones, the broader the tonal range. Some special high-contrast photographs have no tonal range and skip from stark white to pure black.

Tonal rendition. The reproduction of the gray tones of a negative's tonal range. Tonal rendition is said to be good if the tonal range achieved from a normal negative is considered broad.

Tonal scale. Another name for the gray scale used with the *Zone system.*

Tonal separation. The visible difference between the gray tones of a photograph.

Toning. Dyeing a black and white photograph for a special effect. Toners can be used to make the paper appear colder or warmer and also to color the background a variety of shades.

Top light. See *Hairlight.*

Transmission. The measure of the rate at which light will pass through a negative.

Transparency. A color or black and white film positive, which can be mounted in a frame and enlarged with a projector. Also called a slide.

Transport mechanism. The sprocketed reels used to move the film across the film plane smoothly and evenly. The transport mechanism is part of the *take-up spool.*

Tri-color filter. A filter that contains three colors to allow for special effect filtering and tri-colors in color photography.

Tripack. An early name for the triple-layer color films. See under *Subtractive process.*

Triple condenser. An optical system used in some enlargers to direct the light from the lamp through the condenser.

Tripod. Three-legged camera support. A tripod is used when movement is critical, such as when working with a very long lens, in close-up photography, and in copy work.

Tri-X. Trademark for a high-speed black and white film manufactured by Kodak and rated at 400 ASA.

Tungsten lighting. Normal indoor lighting from an incandescent bulb.

Twin-lens reflex camera. A type of camera with two lenses—one for focusing the subject and the other for producing the image on film. Because the twin lens reflex camera has a fixed mirror to reflect the light for focusing, the ground glass is located at the top of the camera. Focusing is done at waist level by looking directly down at the camera. Twin-lens reflex cameras hold a larger (2¼) size film and are bulkier than the popular 35 mm camera.

2¼ camera. One that takes photographs on film with exposures that measure 2¼ × 2¼ inches. Most 2¼ cameras are twin-lens reflexes, although there are several single-lens reflex models on the market today.

2¼ film. A large-format roll film with exposures that measure 2¼ × 2¼ inches.

Two-bath formulation. A type of film developer that requires two solutions to produce the image.

2 × extender. A tele-extender that can double the magnification power of a lens, creating a longer focal length.

Type A color film. Film that has an emulsion which is balanced for use with photoflood lighting.

Type B color film. Film that has an emulsion which is balanced for use with professional tungsten lighting.

Ultraviolet. The portion of the electromagnetic spectrum just beyond visible light on the blue, or shorter wavelength, end. Ultraviolet light, while invisible to the human eye, affects photographic films to the same extent as visible light.

Ultraviolet filter. See *UV filter.*

Umbrella. A collapsible dome-shaped reflector used to *bounce* the light from an electronic flash gun.

Underwater housing. A clear plastic water-tight case used to carry a camera underwater. This type of housing allows a photographer to take pictures at fairly great depths.

Universal carrier. A type of negative carrier that holds several different size films.

UV filter. Stands for Ultraviolet Filter. A special filter used to absorb ultraviolet radiation and reduce haze in long-distance outdoors shots. When used in the mountains, at high altitudes, or from airplanes, ultraviolet filters improve the tonal rendition and contrast in black and white photography and reduce the excess blue in color photography. Also called a haze filter.

Vacuum frame. See *Vacuum table.*

Vacuum table. A device used to hold film securely in place for exposure in either a copy camera or a contact printing frame. A vacuum table consists of a motorized suction base and a tight-fitting glass top. Some vacuum tables allow exposure through the top for contact printing, while others are mounted directly on the large copy cameras used to make halftones for the graphic arts industry. Also called a vacuum frame.

Value. A gray tone reproduced in a black and white print. The *Zone system* is based on a range of tones, or values, between black and white.

Variable contrast paper. Photographic printing paper that is used with a variety of magenta and yellow filters to produce a wide range of contrasts with one emulsion. Also called multicontrast paper.

Variable focus lens. See *Zoom lens.*

View camera. The large, bulky camera used for studio portraiture. View cameras accommodate a variety of large film formats, including 4 × 5 inch and 8 × 10 inch sheet film negatives. The standard view camera is not much different today than it was almost a hundred years ago. Focusing is still done directly on the ground glass with a black cloth draped over the head. Fine focusing aids are often used with the larger format cameras.

View finder. An eyepiece mounted on the back of small cameras, which allows the photographer to see the picture in terms of the film's dimensions. In single-lens reflex cameras and coupled range-finders, focusing is done through the view finder.

Viewing screen. The ground glass of the camera on which the image may be viewed and focused. Also called a focusing screen or simply ground glass.

Vignetting. Cutting the corners off an image. Vignetting may be intentional (it is often used for effect) or the fault of some close-up attachments.

Viscose sponge. A special type of sponge used to wipe film after washing. The viscose sponge absorbs a great deal of water without leaving fibers on the wet emulsion.

Voltage regulator. An electric device used to control the current passing through an outlet into an enlarger. This current must be precisely regulated for color printing because fluctuations in voltage can cause variations in the color temperature of the enlarger light and disrupt color balance. Also called a voltage stabilizer.

Voltage stabilizer. See *Voltage regulator.*

Waist-level view finder. A ground glass that faces upward and which must be held at about waist level for focusing most pictures. Waist-level view finders are generally bulky and inconvenient but can come in handy for close-up work or for pictures of children or animals in which the camera is rested directly on the floor or ground.

Warm tone paper. Photographic paper with a slight ivory cast to the paper base, creating an impression of warmth.

Washing. Running water over film and prints to remove all traces of fixer. If film or paper is not properly washed, streaking and chemical contamination can occur. Improperly washed prints smell strongly of fixer and turn brown in a very short time. Film will be blotchy and streaky.

Waterhouse f-stops. A fixed aperture positioned between the lens elements. Because of the static position, in-between f/stops, or half-stops, are impossible. There is no interleaved diaphragm in a lens with Waterhouse f/stops.

Watt-seconds. A measurement of the storage capacity of the condenser in an electronic flash unit.

Wavelength. The distance light travels to complete one full, undulating phase. Aside from the technical definition, the most important aspect of wavelength is that each color of light has a different wavelength, with red being the longest and blue the shortest.

White light data. Information printed on a box of color printing paper to indicate the individual difference in color balance of that batch of paper. White light data include the densities of color correction filters needed to achieve a proper balance and the ex. factor, which indicates the emulsion's sensitivity.

Wide-angle lens. A camera lens with a broader viewing field than the human eye. Extremely wide-angle lenses, called fish-eye lenses, can view a full 180 degrees. In general, wide-angle lenses can be used to take pictures of a wide subject in a tight area. The visual distortions of a wide-angle lens are exactly the opposite of those in a telephoto lens; instead of compressing space, a wide-angle lens will seem to deepen it. This will cause objects to appear farther away from the camera than they really are and alter size relations so that objects close to the lens appear abnormally large. One advantage of the deepened space is an increase in depth of field. Also called a short-focus lens.

Winder. See *Power winder.*

Wratten 3 safelight. Trademark for an amber safelight used in a darkroom.

X-sync. Shortened term for *X-synchronization.*

X-synchronization. The marking on the shutter-speed dial that causes the shutter to operate in unison with an electronic flash. X-syncs are particularly necessary in cameras with focal-plane shutters. If the shutter speed is not set slow enough, the brief flash will illuminate only one strip of the frame instead of the full frame.

Yellow. One of the primaries used in processing of color slides and prints. The other two primaries are cyan (blue) and magenta (red).

Zone system. A system developed by Ansel Adams and used to determine the proper exposure of a picture based on a series of gray tonal values. These gray values, or scales, are divided into ten distinct tones ranging from pure white to solid black. In the Zone system, the photographer exposes for the range of tones he wishes in the finished print. This may not be an average reading and may in some cases eliminate many of the middle or extreme tones, depending on the desired effect.

Zoom lens. One which has the capacity of producing several focal lengths. A zoom lens is an elaborate combination of elements set up so that there is an infinite number of focal lengths between the shortest and longest lengths of the lens. This is accomplished by several moving elements inside the lens. Because the lens elements move, not all the aberrations can be successfully controlled in all the positions. Also known as a variable focus lens or (take a deep breath) a continuously variable focal length lens.